Manic Depression

At Close Quarters

Author

Barry Hardy

I live in a magnificent body now that I know how to support its needs

Manic Depression At Close Quarters

Copyright © 2009 Barry Hardy publications which is part of BH Management Services Ltd, London UK

The pre launch version of this book was published 06th February 2009 in Great Britain with First Edition published 20th February 2009.

All rights reserved. No part of this book may be reproduced or transmitted in any form or by any means without written permission of the author.

ISBN 978-0-9561538-1-4

Discover more at www.barryhardy.com

At the point I began to understand my realities I knew my life would change

DECENCY WARNING

Please note that Manic Depression At Close Quarters contains strong, explicit views including the use of offensive language, which some may find unnecessarily gratuitous. Therefore please don't read this book if you are easily offended by:

- Strong views.
- Strong language.
- Grammatical inconsistencies.

Or

- Personal experiences and perceptions expressed freely.

I have a magnificent body that supports me in all my endeavours

DEDICATION

This book is dedicated to the battalions of helpless souls butchered in the killing fields of medical man. We who survive will do our level best to right their wrongs. *Manic Depression at Closes Quarters was written and complied entirely in a multicultural internet café in south London and I thank my hosts profoundly for their unequivocal generosity and continued support of my endeavours on this front.*

At the point I began to understand my realities I knew my life would change

Disclaimer

The information provided in this book should not be construed as personal medical or clinical advice or instruction no action should be taken based solely on the contents of this book. Readers should consult appropriate professionals on any matter relating to their health and well being. The information and opinions provided here are for personal research purposes only. Readers who fail to consult appropriate professionals assume the risk of incurring injury and must accept any consequences directly or indirectly associated with their personal actions on any and all related matters.

I have a magnificent body that supports me in all my endeavours

Foreword

Chronic Manic Depression is real and what's more it's truly an insidious condition that invades and destroys every aspect of everything that we as mortals, should care to value. It erodes our sense of self, our sense of hope; in fact it erodes the very essence of living a happy, fulfilled and productive life. I know only too well the sheer hell that is; undiagnosed chronic illness including the heavy load it imposes upon our lives. You see, I had an unqualified disease over a 30+ year period that pushed me into a state of chronic illness, fatigue and depression that was beyond belief, so dreadful and so black that the thought of release through death was my only yet constant companion. Today I often wonder just how it was that I was brave enough, strong enough and pragmatic enough to solve the mystery of that condition. Whilst those charged with the responsibility of aiding and helping me, simply sat back on their ignorant behinds or placed the blame for my condition back onto me. Unsurprising really when all things are considered, because the plain fact of the matter is that the medical industry by default, despite any and all protestations to the contrary, simply doesn't understand chronic illness and simply doesn't care about anyone in its care. The result of which is that it is us as that industries employers, who inevitably suffer as a result of all its mortal failings, prejudices, scientific ignorance and underperformance on a global scale. To fully understand the sheer depths of

At the point I began to understand my realities I knew my life would change

suffering that I endured to acquire myself healing and self management knowledge you should perhaps read my foundation book *Raphael's Legacy published in 2008.* For in that book I cover many aspects of my own personal pursuit of well being as well as publicly denouncing the fraudulent myth's and prejudices within our medical model that result in so much misdiagnosis and medical/clinical underperformance on a global scale. Before we go any further together on this journey I need to make you clear about one very important point; you see, although I find myself writing this self help book. Actually I have absolutely no medical qualifications and/or medical training; however I do have enough intellect and chronic illness expression experience to be eminently qualified enough to voice my opinions upon how to investigate, treat and remove from our lives what is an indiscriminately cancerous condition. You see, chronic illness expression in the vast majority of instances does not originate from insanity or emotional instability despite;

- Any and all claims by the medical/clinical industry that they are the only true generators of the chronic illness expression.

Or

- Any and all current or formative neuro-linguistic programming that reinforces the point that insanity or emotional instability are the only true generators of the chronic illness expression.

I have a magnificent body that supports me in all my endeavours

Because

- Only bodily disease, bodily system/process failures, issues with your endocrine system or chronic inflammation can propagate, promote and / or generate symptoms of chronic illness expression and that as far as I am concerned is FACT.

At the point I began to understand my realities I knew my life would change

ACKNOWLEDGMENTS

My sincere thanks go out to:

My lovely Karina without who's love and support for and of me there would have been no mortal redemption or hope for me.

Dr Sarah Myhill and Hania Baker for all their support and generosity towards my wellbeing and clinical care.

Mrs Edna Garrick for her generosity in agreeing to proof read my manuscript for me.

Mr Abdi Nur Ali, Mr. Dahir Nur Ali and Mr Abdikarin Mohamed for their generosity during the compilation of this book in their internet café on Westow Hill.

Finally to all the medical / clinical incompetents that I've encountered thus far, you are the only reason for this books production. I always knew that there was an answer to my problem and having proved that I'm now happy to share it with the world.

I have a magnificent body that supports me in all my endeavours

ESSENTIAL READING

Everything covered in this book draws upon my own detailed personal passage through chronic illness that I cover in my book *Raphael's Legacy*. To ensure that you understand and / or do not either misinterpret or misrepresent any statement, phrase or passage in this book, please ensure that you have read Raphael's Legacy prior to exploring the subtle nuances of this book. In that way you can ensure that you fully understand why I say the things I say and why I propose the things in the way that I propose them in this book. For your reference a listing of all Raphael's Legacy derivative support books are at your disposal on the next page. Finally and above all things, please ensure that as you move towards better health always ensure that you are adequately supported by a suitably qualified professional service provider.

At the point I began to understand my realities I knew my life would change

Further personal insight and self help books written by Barry Hardy in relation to Raphael's Legacy include:

Raphael Treatment Protocol
Stress at Close Quarters
Anxiety at Close Quarters
Exploring Fluid Normality
Arthritis at Close Quarters
Depression at Close Quarters
Fibromyalgia at Close Quarters
Lymes Disease at Close Quarters
Gulf War Syndrome at Close Quarters
Toxic Body Syndrome at Close Quarters
Myalgic Encephalopathy at Close Quarters
Chronic Fatigue Syndrome at Close Quarters
Obsessive Compulsive Disorder at Close Quarters

You can purchase any of these books at www.barryhardy.com

I have a magnificent body that supports me in all my endeavours

At the point I began to understand my realities I knew my life would change

CONTENTS

Decency warning 3
Dedication 4
Disclaimer 5
Foreword 6
Acknowledgments 9
Essential reading 10
Contents 13
Exploration introduction 15
Exploration of clinical manic depression......................... 23
Exploring the journey into darkness pragmatically 27
Exploring the darker side of medicine pragmatically 39
Exploring psychological illness pragmatically 47
Exploring lymes disease pragmatically 63
Exploring genetic time bomb links pragmatically 75
Exploring physiological stress pragmatically 87
Exploring depression expression pragmatically 117

I have a magnificent body that supports me in all my endeavours

Exploring obsessive compulsive disorder pragmatically 159
Exploring analytical testing pragmatically 173
Exploring analytical testing options pragmatically 195
Exploring personal mind anger pragmatically 201
Exploring your current diagnosis pragmatically 209
Authors notes 223
Web sites you may wish to explore 229
Other books by barry hardy 230
Decency Warning 231

At the point I began to understand my realities I knew my life would change

EXPLORATION INTRODUCTION

Exploration One

I have a magnificent body that supports me in all my endeavours

At the point I began to understand my realities I knew my life would change

If you're currently suffering from and/or have suffered from Manic Depression in the past and wish to unravel the truth about everything associated with that expression of disease. Then perhaps it's understandable why you arrived at your decision to read this book. But what you may not know yet is, this book like all my self help books is based upon my own personal approach to illness expression on the firm understanding that I'm certainly no guru or medically/clinically qualified individual. I'm just a regular guy who ignored my doubters and abusers and took my conditions head on until I was able to qualify my conditions root cause via scientific analysis. Therefore if you're interested in exploring my views all I would ask is that you:

(a) Stay open and consider fully any and all of the postulations I explore in this book for the pursuit of well-being, before deciding upon the most appropriate approach or course of action for you.

And

(b) Always work with or at least consult with; a suitably qualified service provider before making changes to any or all of your current treatment protocols.

Let's not beat around the bush then; as I'm sure you're aware Manic Depression is such an invasive state of existence, for when you are in its grasp, nothing makes sense and all seems to be pain, for in that place you live a life which seems void of hope. But the reality is that where there is life, there is always hope, for where there is hope, there is always the potential for renewal and growth. The essence of my personal renewal and growth was nothing more than tenacity in the midst of seemingly insurmountable odds. Bolstered only by a desire to prove my

I have a magnificent body that supports me in all my endeavours

antagonists wrong and to reduce where possible the struggle or struggles of any of my fellow men. I believe that; 'anything and everything is possible with the right skills, the right people and the right approach' and in that mind set I proved how to rid myself of chronic illness. During that process I learned who failed me and why they failed me, who chose to ignore me and why they chose to ignore me, but I also learned who truly loved me with all their heart and why they loved me with all their heart and that is the true beauty of success over intense adversity. We all have the potential to recover from chronic illness, no matter what form it takes e.g. Manic Depression. That is if we're truly prepared to accept that we can recover, but if we choose not to recover from chronic illness then we make that choice for the personal reasons that only we know best. I made a firm choice to recover from chronic illness expression and in compiling this book I'm now offering you the tools, understanding and insight to recover from your own chronic condition too i.e. Manic Depression . In committing to my own personal recovery I explored many many things and that's why it's easy for me to acknowledge and pronounce out loud that:

- To those who failed me, who criticised me, who ridiculed me, to those who misdiagnosed me, who mistreated me and who clinically abused me I say to you now: may your god forgive you for all that you are for you are without doubt the lowest of all mortal life forms.

At the point I began to understand my realities I knew my life would change

- To those who could have, should have, yet chose not to heed me, to help me, to support me or to love me I say to you now, do not attempt to re-write my past by reaching out and connecting with me now or in the future. It's not for me to forgive you your prejudices, your ignorance, your selfishness or your cruelty towards me. As a mortal I merely wish for you strength, growth and rebirth as you pass through your own personal hells that I believe lay before you.

- To those who loved me, who prayed for me, who laughed with me, who cried with me and to those who died with me many times I say to you now; we may be few, but we are the luckiest of all living things. We have loved, we have cared, we have given, we have shared, we have lived and we will die touched by the presence of unquestionable friends.

I firmly believe that you as a sufferer of Manic Depression need to look at the bit and big players in your life for in doing so you will allow yourself to move forward quicker than you ever thought possible. You see; the process to wellness starts completely with a considered acceptance of your past in unison with you future expectations because that and only that approach to life brings forth new ways of being, new ways of thinking and implicitly new ways of living. A life filled with fun and free from manufactured fear or ignorantly propagated prejudices or misrepresentation of scientific fact. Because the very simple FACT is that Manic Depression always originates from:

1. Physical diseases and/or rarely injury to the brain.

Or

I have a magnificent body that supports me in all my endeavours

2. Bodily process failure and/or deviations from normal functioning.

Or

3. Inflammation generated through diseases or injury.

Or

4. Toxic body syndrome generated through, physical disease, bodily process failure and/or deviations from normal functioning and inflammation generated through diseases or injury.

At the point I began to understand my realities I knew my life would change

Now I realise that the points I've made thus far may be a lot for anyone suffering from chronic illness in whatever form that takes to come to terms initially given the general level of perceptional and medical/clinical clap trap surrounding chronic illness. All I can say is that you the reader will always be able to validate or disregard my postulations in relation to your particular illness at the point you've given due consideration to all I have to say. Living with any form of chronic illness is neither right, nor acceptable in any way shape or form and at the point you're free from its deadly expression in your lives, you will again realise why mortality can be such an enriching and simply mind blowing undertaking. I hope that this book changes your views upon Manic Depression, because unlike any other book on Manic Depression. This book will postulate alternative slants on aspects of chronic illness generation, hence opening up new ways of thought, new ways of seeing and new ways of dealing with your chronic Manic Depression. Because once we have at our disposal all the information we need to secure better health, the entire picture and road to recovery becomes so much clearer.

You see, we all have the power to take control of our lives and to live in the way that we choose to live. For in committing to that way of being we are actually setting ourselves free of any of the negative programming we've inherited that has played a big part in compromising our perceptions upon life. We have the right to be all that we were ever born to be, and that means being free always from disease and ignorant prejudices about disease which in reality only hold us back.

I have a magnificent body that supports me in all my endeavours

On that very point I now invite you to explore my thoughts, views and suggestions designed to eradicate Manic Depression from your lives and sincerely hope at the very least they open up a new avenue of hope for you.

At the point I began to understand my realities I knew my life would change

Exploration of clinical manic depression

Exploration Two

I have a magnificent body that supports me in all my endeavours

At the point I began to understand my realities I knew my life would change

What is there to say about Manic Depression save for the fact that anyone who suffers from it knows truly just how difficult morality can be. Because sufferers of Manic Depression somehow have to come to terms with chronic and unrelenting Manic Depression, depression and/or an inability to simply cope, which impact upon the normality of mortality in every way shape and form. Manic Depression saps resolve and pushes it's sufferers to and beyond seemingly unimaginable points of despair. But the worst thing of all is that populist and medical/clinical perceptions of Manic Depression is; that it's somehow just a manifestation of deep seated psychological and/or psychiatric issues.

But actually I find the perception of Manic Depression strange to say the very least because when you think about it or ask anyone from the medical/clinical world. No one is actually able or prepared to qualify actually what Manic Depression is, over and above that is the bog standard clap trap we've all heard so many times about our psychology being able to manifest disease in all shapes and forms and when we sort our head out, hooray we become Manic Depression free. Well the plain and simple fact of that matter is that Manic Depression is a disease generated symptom, therefore if we wish to make any improvement we need to:

(a) Identify which disease is generating the manifestation of Manic Depression symptomology.

And

(b) Develop a holistic treatment protocol where eradication and not suppression of symptomology remains key.

I have a magnificent body that supports me in all my endeavours

I'm now going to explore a whole raft of issues which I hope stimulate insight for you, because I actually believe that it's eminently possible to solve personal Manic Depression battles when our search for the truth remains firmly focused upon root cause analysis. With that position very much to the fore, I'm going to cover aspects of my healing process against horrendous odds whilst also hopefully enlightening you on some or the more darker sides of medical/clinical failures of due diligence.

At the point I began to understand my realities I knew my life would change

EXPLORING THE JOURNEY INTO DARKNESS PRAGMATICALLY

Exploration Three

At the point I began to understand my realities I knew my life would change

My decline into chronic ill health and intense chronic illness expression resulted from over three decades of medical/clinical abuse and neglect and you can read more about that in my book *Raphael's Legacy*. Nevertheless as a guy who's been through a horrific state of undiagnosed disease I realise now that the fall from good health into that of a chronic diseased state is not always a straight forward process and can take many years. The thing is we have nothing without good health, no prosperity, no career or joy, yet good health is something we all take for granted until it's ripped forever from our grasp. As a society we're not programmed to explore and look for answers when our health is in decline, because we absolve ourselves of that responsibility and empower only a select few. Therein we lose the connection that we need to plot and determine the origin and cause of our disease because as our body's sole custodian we ultimately hold all the answers and that is the only true key to recovery. As part of the foundation work required to support my diseased state postulation it was important for me in the preparation of my book *Raphael's Legacy* that I mapped and shared with you my own personal health decline, for in that process all the connections are clearly defined. With a simple red line mapping depression expression, a blue line mapping physical strength and green line mapping my emotional strength over an entire forty year period.

I have a magnificent body that supports me in all my endeavours

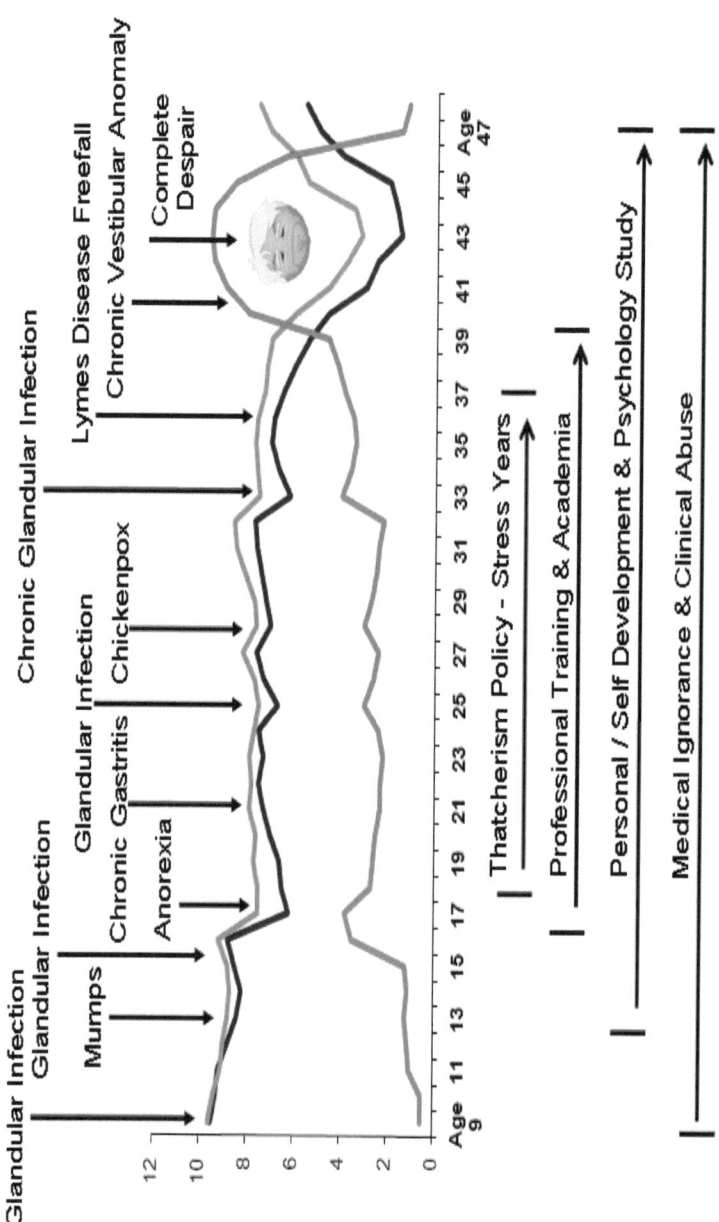

At the point I began to understand my realities I knew my life would change

Before I elaborate further upon my own health decline however it's important that I cover emotional and depressive state perceptions because they are frequently cited by medical charlatans as the originators of illness. When in reality they are nothing more than an expression of disease. Nevertheless there is a big difference between emotional state and depressive state and they must never be confused or directly linked as one in the same because they are not, *but I will qualify this point further in subsequent chapters.* Our emotional state in essence is our ability to cope, to rise to a challenge, to pick ourselves up after a set back and/or to project ourselves into the future and is nothing more than a derivative of our endocrine functionality.

Whereas depression I'm prepared to argue is nothing more than a symptom of disease and should not therefore be confused with subtle mood swings which are part of our normal emotional expressions. As you will observe my health profile map starts way back at the point of formalized body awareness for me where I'm aware that I had exceptionally high levels of physical endurance and emotional strength with low depression intent i.e. I simply coped, laughed and joked. Those expressions are mapped such that, physical and emotional scores at ten indicate high energy levels and equally very strong emotional stability. Whereas zero would indicate that I have no energy, no resilience, no emotional rigidity, no fight, in essence I'm simply burnt out. In terms of depression expression, zero on the map indicates no depression present whereas ten would indicate chronic suicidal depression. As my health declined it's easy to see the correlation between physical strength and emotional strength and the impact that disease has upon all three states i.e. physical and emotional states decline in vitality and depression increases with paradoxical ferocity during chronic disease. Therefore my primary postulation is that the vast majority of depressive states are a direct result

I have a magnificent body that supports me in all my endeavours

of a diseased state and that depression is not the generator of illness as most medics would have us believe. Depression in itself is not an illness in the vast majority of cases; rather it is merely a symptom that simply manifests through disease. Equally; psychological stress is not the originator of fatigue at best it is merely a bit player or derivative of the same diseased state. It is therefore very important that we all understand that the originator of chronic symptomology is not the fault of the patient it is nothing more than an indicator of disease. Understand that and you're at least part of the way to accepting that you have a condition in Manic Depression which needs treating and that you're not the entire cause of all your presenting symptoms.

In the absence of medical/clinical scientific intellect, my battle for resolution from chronic illness expression took me to places where I would hope no fellow mortal should ever have to go. It cost me my career, my prosperity, my homes and ultimately could have cost me my life had I not been blessed with a little bit of luck and a body and mind that refused to be written off. After three decades of suffering and at a cost of over 300k I was diagnosed with Lyme's Disease, but that process despite all the self sacrifice it required on a physical, emotional, spiritual and financial level, gave birth to a man who now knows:

1. The truth about our medical/clinical industry, all it's failing, ignorance and lack of scientific validity!

And

2. What is needed on the part of any mortal to get well from a whole host of hitherto so called untreatable or so called psychological conditions!

At the point I began to understand my realities I knew my life would change

Manic Depression At Close Quarters 33

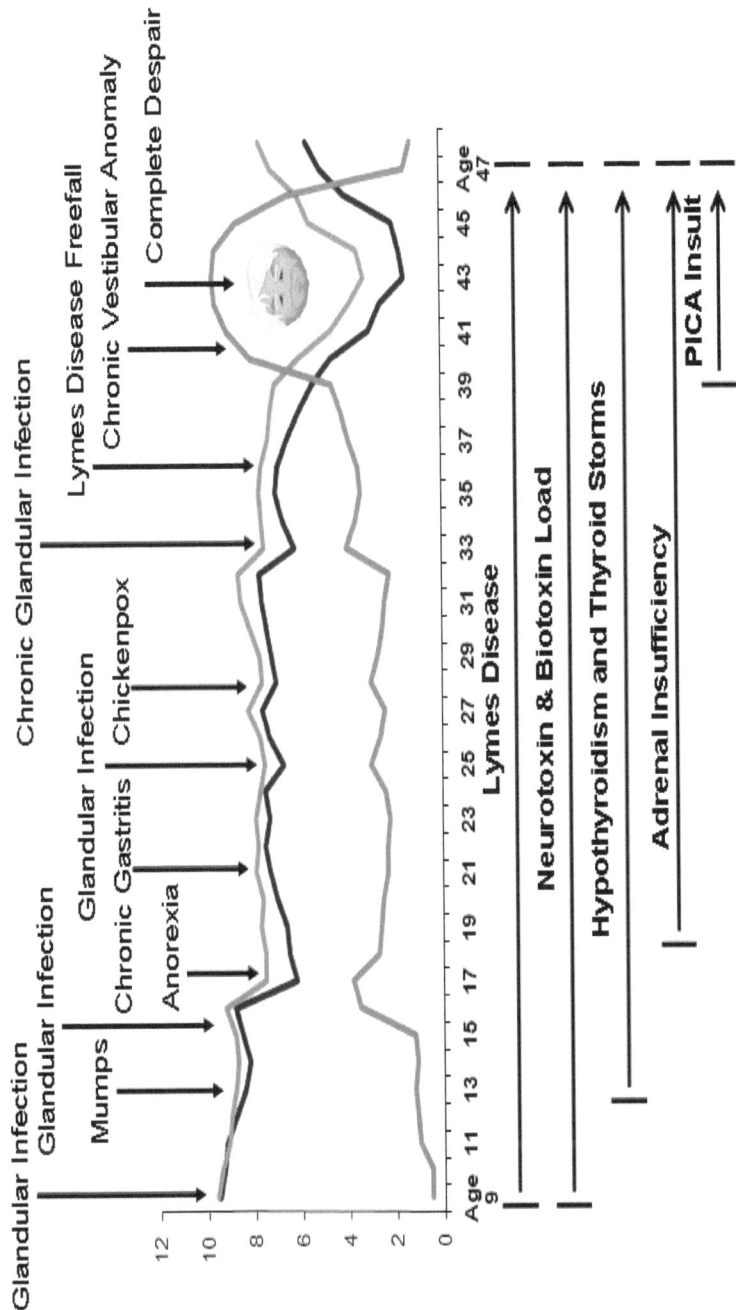

I have a magnificent body that supports me in all my endeavours

In pursuit of my own personal well being I discovered that:

- I contacted Lymes Disease at a very young age the impact of which was that it compromised my liver, my brain and my endocrine system re: *Raphael's Legacy*

- My bodily systems were simply unable to cope with that untreated load and so over the years battling to solve my body's infection, my body simply burnt itself out, re: *Raphael's Legacy*

- When exposed to even higher levels of Lymes Disease my limited defenses were simply overrun and my health simply went into freefall and I moved very quickly into a rampant Lymes Diseased state and toxic body syndrome, re: *Raphael's Legacy*

- A situation compounded still further by the chronic activation of a simply horrendous vascular vestibular insult which was completely poo poo'd by the medical / clinical charlatans that I saw until I was able to prove its origin via self-funded imaging and neurosurgery re: *Raphael's Legacy*.

At the point I began to understand my realities I knew my life would change

Now the question is;

Are you open enough, ready enough and / or willing enough to explore your own chronic illness state of Manic Depression from a whole new perspective in an attempt to move both it and you into a new holistic place of considered and greater understanding?

If so;

Then take a deep breath and prepare for a bumpy yet hopefully rewarding ride, because some of the material I'm going to cover from now on in this book may simply shock you to your core.

But hey:

That's okay and I'm sure you'll agree otherwise you wouldn't be reading this book right now would you?

I have a magnificent body that supports me in all my endeavours

What you may ask has all this got to do with Manic Depression? Well the answer is, not one single medic or clinician helped me when I was being destroyed by a horrendous disease despite that fact that my chronic illness levels were as chronic as it's possible to be. All they ever did was write me off at worst and at best offer me, medications that offered no resolution or hope for me. The plain disagreeable fact of the matter is that there are no medics or clinicians out there who remotely understand disease or Manic Depression which means that we're completely devoid of help at the point our body moves into a chronic diseased state. What's even worse is that by the time our bodies decline into a chronic diseased state the root cause of our disease on our records is so hidden or masked by psychological inaccuracies or simply medical clap trap that the possibility of securing an effective diagnosis is in reality highly remote. I know of far too many people myself included who've been tortured by disease and ultimately chronic illness expression who've been ignored and abused wholesale by the medical/clinical world through dogma, ignorance and incompetence in terms of trying to find a scientific solution to our disease state conditions, to such an extent that it's an absolute bloody scandal. A situation which directly forced me to explore why it was that the medical/clinical world was so reluctant to help people in despair and what needed to change to bring about greater receptivity.

At the point I began to understand my realities I knew my life would change

During my endeavours on this matter I found only to my great annoyance that the medical/clinical industries including everyone who either works in it or supports it are simply:

- Happy with underperformance and shoddy service delivery.

- Happy to continually write its customer base off whilst continuously seeking to self elevate its/their own status through bullshit and medical/clinical ignorance and dogma.

It is an industry;

- So locked in inertia that its own scientific base is at least one hundred years ahead of its own front end service provision.

Now I'm in no way saying that in order to recover from Manic Depression we all must plot our decline in health similar to the detail that I myself was forced to do so, to enable me to pass though my horrendous and deep black hole. But what I am saying is that there is a need for a significant change in our perceptions about the way we currently perceive poor health and in particular chronic Manic Depression because without that; there is very little potential for symptom free resolution and long term recovery. Therefore the key to freedom from self destruct or medical/clinical abuse in terms of Manic Depression is to always remember that chronic illness expression no matter what form it takes is always the result of anyone or all of the following:

1. Physical diseases.
2. Rarely injury to the brain.
3. Bodily process failure and/or deviations from normal functioning.
4. Inflammation generated through diseases.
5. Inflammation generated through injury to the brain.
6. Toxic body syndrome generated through, physical disease, bodily process failure and/or deviations from normal functioning and inflammation generated through diseases or injury.

At the point I began to understand my realities I knew my life would change

Exploring the darker side of medicine pragmatically

Exploration Four

I have a magnificent body that supports me in all my endeavours

At the point I began to understand my realities I knew my life would change

You may be surprised to read this, but let me send a shock wave racing right through your body because I'm going to empower you with a very distasteful truth. You see, at the point you move into a state of chronic ill health and/or Manic Depression the deadliest people you will ever meet are those who work within and/or who support the medical/clinical world.

So much so that I'm somewhat embarrassed these days by the fact that whilst many turned their back during the greedy and wasted Thatcher and Major years. I spent a great deal of my youth campaigning and lobbying against local and central government with passion on a whole host of issues, not least to save what I felt was a laudable institution under threat, namely our glorious NHS. 'Boy did I get it wrong'. The institution and all the mechanisms that underpin that bullshit ridden and sedentary industry are rotten to the core.

Fortunately I have no medical or clinical qualifications, I'm just a regular guy trained in engineering and engineering sciences and like most engineers I have an engaging and problem solving mind. As a regular guy, albeit with a little bit of professional training, I would respectfully suggest that having an enquiring, capable and problem solving mind is probably the most rudimentary of all mandatory requirements for all those engaged in a key service delivery profession such as the medical industry. Now clearly the back room girls and boys of that industry appear to have that predisposition because we have all witnessed the tremendous advances that have been achieved over the past fifty years or so. I'm talking here however about medical scientists and scientific medical engineers, the people we should regard as the true heroes of medicine, the men and woman who steadfastly develop new tools, new tests, new treatments, new techniques and new machines etc, for the betterment of man. However, the heroes of medicine are a stark contrast

I have a magnificent body that supports me in all my endeavours

to the front end 'luddites' i.e. *Any Opponent of Industrial Change or Innovation* of the medical world that we the general public are unfortunately exposed to. The people that we're exposed to are only interested in one thing and one thing only: self gratification at the expense of their fellow man. I refer of course to the medical receptionist, the nurse, the general practitioner, the registrar, the specialist and the consultant. They may or may not start off life as self protectionist 'luddites' but at the point they're allowed to administer their own unique brand of divisive, destructive and judgmental clinical administration and medical butchery up the innocent public, they move into that 'luddite' mindset wholesale.

These people are guilty of crimes against humanity that simply eclipse the acts and transgressions of the worst of all ruthless dictators. They are institutionally lazy, self obsessed, greedy, serial abusers with only one thing on their agenda, self preservation of their highly inflated status within what is the devil's own institutions. Forget any waffle about the Hippocratic oath that anyone from this industry chooses to offload onto you, the bottom line for these people is themselves first, themselves second and whatever is left over; is all for themselves. These people don't solve problems, they don't hear suffering, they're not prepared to think outside of the box and why? Well because they're the wrong people for the job, the wrong people who are gaining great rewards from an industry that is rotten to the core. For anyone misfortunate enough to develop a chronic illness I've mapped the actual clinical abuse process that most people are forced to endure during the course of their chronic illness at the end of this chapter. What the process loop cannot do is qualify the simply appalling nature, neglect and abandonment anyone experiences during that process. Where the cause of desperate conditions are often written off as psychological issues and placed

At the point I began to understand my realities I knew my life would change

directly back on the shoulders of the patients, identifying them as the originator and hence owner of the condition in totality. That being said; it's eminently justifiable to suggest that the selection criteria for individuals entering the medical industry and the training they undergo are now by modern day standards both outdated and fundamentally flawed. Because if the selection criteria for those entering the medical industry and their subsequent training were right; then we wouldn't have such a fundamentally flawed service and individuals who go onto develop chronic Manic Depression wouldn't simply be written off. You only need to be misfortunate enough to become ill to discover just how diabolically poor, unresponsive and uncooperative this industry really is. No matter which sector you seek help from, be it either the public or the private sectors, the service is abominable. No matter whom you consult or what level that representative may be, it doesn't matter what tests you participate in or what sort of investigation you undergo. These people know very little about very little and what they do know or articulate freely to you is generally outdated, self protectionist and complete and utter rubbish with no humanistic element to it. You see:

- How can it be that we still have a sociologically biased industry that is controlled from within?

- How can it be that we still have a sociologically biased industry that protects and rewards underperformance from those who support it or are employed by it?

- How can it be that we still have a sociologically biased industry that is afraid to acknowledge advancement in thinking until that change in approach is decades old?

I have a magnificent body that supports me in all my endeavours

- How can it be that we still have a sociologically biased industry where those who are employed in it have no idea about the majority of diseases and conditions they encounter?

- How can it be that every unexplainable condition can be written off by those within this industry as simply being of a psychological origin?

- How can it be that they're programmed as a service provider within this industry not to hear, help or support suffering and pain?

- How can it be that no matter what your own personal or professional credentials are, as soon as you engage with this industry you're immediately considered an intellectual cretin by those providing basic services within?

- How can it be that if you dare to challenge this industry from within you're immediately risking your career?

- How can it be that fighting for resolution from chronic illness can expose you to the pressure of clinical services being withdrawn from you?

At the point I began to understand my realities I knew my life would change

And yet they all assume the same grotesque air of arrogance about who they are and what they are and how complicated your particular situation may or may not be. This bullshit they offload is by default, simply an outdated facade designed for a bygone age when we the general public were considered as intellectually inferior to representation from this industry. But this misguided assumption still exists today to mask clear inadequacies, ignorance and fragile egos yet the reality is that it's probably more disrespectful to us now than it ever was because we're all much smarter than this industry gives us credit for. This crux of my irritation is that this industry and those who support it are an affront to everything that is both decent and good in our modern world. We don't expect or accept bullshit and ridicule from any other private sector or public service industry. So why do we accept this institutional misconduct from the clinical world?

Well, the truth is that we really don't think that we have any power to change our situation and at the point we commence any social intercourse with this industry we're already in a state of vulnerability and low vitality. Therein resides the reason why so many people with undiagnosed disease states go onto to develop chronic Manic Depression before ultimately being written off as a neurotic or a depressive with no possible chance of making an effective recovery. You see the medical/clinical industry is very adept at falsely blaming the symptoms of chronic disease states and ultimately Manic Depression upon the fragile psychology of any mortal who presents with such appalling and life debilitating conditions. But what is the truth behind this predisposition of our psychology being the root cause of all our chronic illness and chronic illness expression? Well I'm going to look at that very point in the next chapter so please fasten your seat belt, but first check out the clinical abuse loop.

I have a magnificent body that supports me in all my endeavours

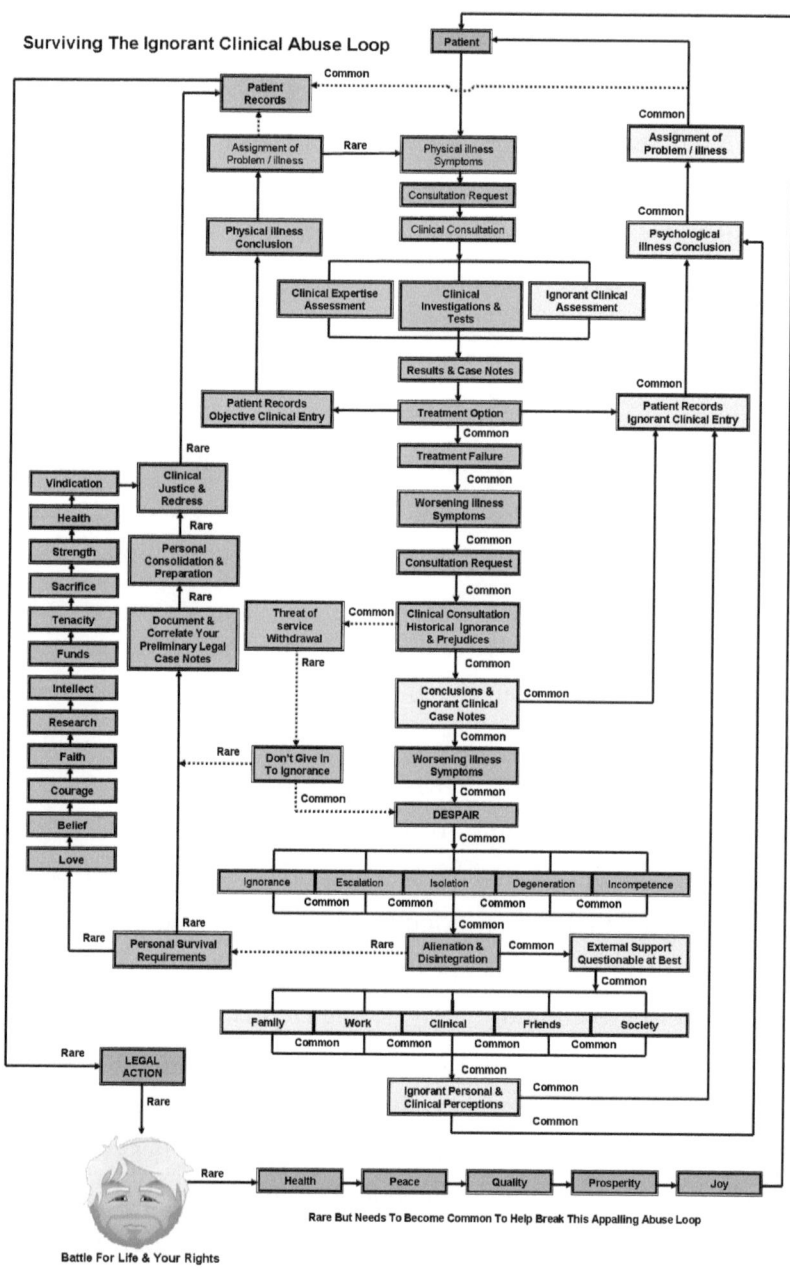

At the point I began to understand my realities I knew my life would change

EXPLORING PSYCHOLOGICAL ILLNESS PRAGMATICALLY

Exploration Five

I have a magnificent body that supports me in all my endeavours

At the point I began to understand my realities I knew my life would change

How frequent is it for patients' problems to be simply written off as nothing more than a deluded psychology? Well far more frequently than you may expect. You see, there is a prescriptive culture within the medical world which has a predisposition for looking to offload all the patients' problems back onto them. It's basically part of the overall clinical abuse model and its guiding principles are no more than:

- When in doubt just call your patients illness a psychological problem.

- When tests don't indicate a deviation from normal values, just call your patients' illnesses a psychological problem.

- When imaging doesn't show up any abnormalities just call your patients' illnesses a psychological problem.

- When you simply can't be bothered with your patients' perceived or preposterous symptoms just call their illness a psychological problem.

I have a magnificent body that supports me in all my endeavours

But what is the truth and just what part does our psychology play in the bigger scheme of things when it comes to our health? Well first we need to understand that whilst we may be familiar with the term 'psychological illness' few of us know that the modern day originator of this scientific field was 'Wilhelm Wundt' who established the first psychology lab in Leipzig, Germany. Believing at the time that *properly* trained individuals should be able to *accurately* identify the mental processes that accompanied an individual's feelings, sensations, and thoughts. The emphasis here is upon *properly trained* individuals accurately identifying the processes that underpin the emotional predisposition of individuals in any given psychological state.

Now the development of this science didn't happen by chance, mankind in all its societies has battled throughout its entire documented history with the thorny issue of mental illness and insanity. That's why we in the United Kingdom still have such draconian measures as the 'Mental Health Act' where citizens can be sectioned and detained under said act for extended periods if they pose either a danger to others or more often than not simply a danger to themselves. Now there is absolutely no doubt that some individuals are insane, we see that in the likes of Shipman, Stalin, Hitler and Saddam Hussein.

The problem is there have been no major advances since time began to delineate between organic insanity and biologically insults that have the propensity to inflict insanity upon mankind. So we still have no way of knowing who's insane and who's simply biologically ill. I'm advocating therefore that the golden psychological card which is so readily used to explain the unexplainable illness i.e. there is a significant psychological component to your illness, is simply a complete red herring in the majority of chronic illnesses.

At the point I began to understand my realities I knew my life would change

Those inaccurate value judgments simply have no clinical grounding upon which to base the assumptions of a psychological condition upon save for some cursory presenting symptoms.

Now it's that point of clinical evidence that I wish firstly to focus upon. You see; if you present yourself to a medic suspecting that you have let's say; possibly hypothyroidism. The first thing they will do is:

(a) Poo poo and ridicule you.

And then

(b) Perhaps agree reluctantly to give you a thyroid test.

They will then rattle on about how they couldn't possibly give you a trial of low dose thyroid medication until your tests results come back and prove that you do indeed have an issue with your thyroid. Yet the same medical practitioner within 5 minutes of another consultation will conclude with NO clinical data that you are indeed suffering from a psychological condition and therein he or she will feel eminently comfortable to prescribe anyone of a line of toxic psychiatric substances. It seems to me incredulous in the 21st century, that some unqualified cretin can make such sweeping statements about the condition of someone's psychology. More so when we realise that we pay these rogues insane salaries for the little that they do. Affording them great status to comply with the values and defining principles of the Hippocratic Oath. But my question is; do they deliver greatness for the greatness we bestow upon them? Well they're certainly paid insane salaries and afforded great status but very few of them have ever actually signed up to any form of; Hippocratic Oath. Furthermore it's fair to suggest that many of them don't actually know what the original Oath actually says despite the fact that they frequently hide behind it.

I have a magnificent body that supports me in all my endeavours

I actually look at that point further in the chapter Hippocratic Oath Or Merely Hypocritical Froth focusing upon specifically all the medical illusions that we as a society are sold.

Nevertheless I'm going to labour my point here of psychological postulation over scientific rationale, by asking this:

- If I have an abscess inside my mouth accompanied by intolerable pain do I have an abscess and intolerable pain?

Or

- Do I have a psychological problem which is manifesting the symptoms of pain?

Well clearly it's the first bullet point not the latter unless that is you're employed in the medical world. You see, in the medical world seeing is not always believing whereas in the presence of no rationale, believing is always right. It is that preoccupation with self importance and unqualified value judgments that continues to blight our medical records and destroy our lives.

But what if I substitute abscess for undetectable anomaly generating misery and great pain that flawed tests and investigations are unable to detect. What do I have then?

- Do I have an undetectable anomaly which is causing misery and pain?

Or

- Do I have a deep seated psychological problem that is manifesting symptoms of misery and pain?

At the point I began to understand my realities I knew my life would change

Well of course it's the latter in terms of medical rationale because; the very fact that my problem cannot be found means that it simply doesn't exist. It must therefore be a manifestation of my fragile psychology which requires no further input from them. Is it any wonder that I regard these rogues as the lowest form of life?

It's clearly apparent to me now that in bog standard, tricky or complex medical investigation situations we the patients are always to a greater extent perceived to be the responsible party for the clinical problem we're experiencing because as mere mortals we have such fragile psychologies. Surely though this situation is truly insane, how can this industry say on one hand that, unless their outdated investigation techniques are able to detect a problem then it simply doesn't exist whilst in the same breath assign clinical labels to patients with the shallowest to zero investigations of their case?

I do not argue or disagree with the fact that our psychology plays a very big part in the way we cope with, or handle our difficulties. But it is not the root cause of all mans hidden or seemingly translucent diseases and I therefore repudiate the waving of the psychological cause golden card by cretins within the medical industry.

If our psychology was the root cause of the majority of illnesses then we would be able to see for ourselves the advances in the treatment of psychological conditions over the past hundred years. Because the money we spend on this aspect of medical care via so called research and residential care etc, is simply insane. The reality to my primary postulation is quite stark and I say that because the medical industry is having a laugh. Nothing much has changed in the diagnosis and treatment of these conditions despite the oceans of scientific papers that have been written.

I have a magnificent body that supports me in all my endeavours

There have been no major breakthroughs in clinical analysis, qualification or treatments of psychological conditions save for commercially sponsored indoctrination and use of debatably successful drugs. Now if anyone who has been put on those drugs has improved, all I can say is good for you, but for the majority of us who didn't need them in our body to solve our health condition, then I would respectfully suggest that they are:

- Dangerous

Or

- Complete waste of bloody time.

Yet the medical world's view remains without any validity that all illness derives from an emotional or mental state and that physical illness if it cannot be pinpointed simply doesn't exist. But surely these are the views of yesterday's men, the sorts who questioned the validity of;

- The shape of the earth.
- The purpose of the sun.
- The make-up of the moon.
- The relevance of the stars

They are the views of men who dared not seek to discover if the world was flat or round and who shouted heresy if a man sort to postulated different thoughts or articulated and challenged perceived truths.

At the point I began to understand my realities I knew my life would change

The very fact that this approach happens almost by default in clinical surgeries throughout the UK, simply validates my position that the medical world is seemingly still stuck in the dark ages, ignorant and despite its protestations, doesn't really care. Were they motor mechanics with the same approach to problems these people would be simply unemployable or even in jail e.g.

- 'I'm sorry Mr. Hardy but I couldn't find anything wrong with your car, but incidentally have you ever tried counselling, sometimes it really does help?'

Or what about this favourite one;

- 'Yes I hear what you say Mr. Hardy but that is just a sensation of knocking at the front of your car, I'm the expert here I can't find any signs of knocking so perhaps its more of a psychological issue than you think, how's your sex life by the way?'

Two months later the engine in my car implodes;

- 'Oh well these things just happen sometimes Mr. Hardy, I've checked your notes and it would appear that your tyres and exhaust were fine when you were last in here, now you're clearly agitated so I'm going to suggest that there seems more to this than just an engine in your car, do you think you need to see a psychiatrist?'

I have a magnificent body that supports me in all my endeavours

- 'Answer, no I don't think I should see a psychiatrist you bull shitting waste of space, I was in here not so long ago and I told you that there was something seriously wrong with my engine and all you did was check my bloody tyre pressure and exhaust mounting. Now I'm back here today with a damaged engine and I'm asking you this, are you a bloody mechanic mate or simply a mechanic on your great grandmothers side of your family because your technical and professional capabilities are shoddy to say the least?'

The thing is if this happened in real life we would be straight to trading standards but when it comes to the medical industry we're all very guilty of not being prepared to take those bastards on. The public at large would be shocked if they knew just how little psychological or psychiatric training non specialists in that field actually undergo before they're let loose on us.

I liken their understanding of psychological or psychiatry to that of the fat clever bastard who we've perhaps sat next to as lovers of football in the football stands all around our country. You know the one I mean. From beginning to end he hurls his abuse and yet he's probably never played the beautiful game. Yet he's somehow deluded himself into thinking that he's some kind of football guru.

Well, the truth is that the average medic you will ever encounter has little to no training in either psychological or matters of psychiatry and as such are the least qualified of clinicians to prescribe conditions of that nature to you or about you. Yet they have bought into ignorant schools of thought which date way back to the 1920's.

At the point I began to understand my realities I knew my life would change

Outdated schools of thought that postulated that we, as individuals, are responsible for all our own thoughts and our perceptions on life and that we all have demons and un-reconciled issues deep within us that frequently manifest themselves as illness. Today that belief is still perpetuated by our ignorant medics as a way of offloading the cause of a tricky problem back onto the shoulders of its originator simply because they know that they can do that.

So much so that you can bet your last £10 that if you encounter any extended or unexplainable medical issue at any point in your life, that the psychological postulations or dogma that will be rolled out or recorded on your medical records will be a derivative of some unqualified cretins understanding of:

- Personality Psychology – This specialist area looks at the various elements that make up individual personalities and includes Freud's structural model of personality as an example of a protagonist of this field.

However at the point a qualified psychologist is brought onto your case I can guarantee you that Personality Psychology which has already been used by medical ignoramuses as ammunition against you will be almost entirely dropped in favour of:

- Clinical Psychology Investigations – This specialty area is focused on the assessment, diagnosis, and treatment of mental disorders.

I have a magnificent body that supports me in all my endeavours

However the study of psychology has moved on tremendously since its conception and there are now many widely differing schools of thought and differing approaches to this challenging subject including:

- Cognitive Psychology - This specialist area is the study of human thought processes and cognitions, including topics such as attention, memory, perception, decision-making, problem solving, and language acquisition.

- Abnormal Psychology - This specialty area is focused on research and treatment of a variety of mental disorders and is linked to psychotherapy and clinical psychology.

- Social Psychology - This specialist area is a discipline that uses scientific methods to study social influence, social perception, and social interaction. Social psychology studies diverse subjects including group behaviour, social perception, leadership, nonverbal behaviour, conformity, aggression, and prejudice.

- Comparative Psychology - This specialist area is the branch of psychology concerned with the study of animal behaviour, believing that the study of animal behaviour can lead to a deeper and broader understanding of human psychology.

- Forensic Psychology - This specialist area is an applied field focused on using psychological research and principles in the legal and criminal justice system.

At the point I began to understand my realities I knew my life would change

- Industrial-Organizational Psychology - This specialist area uses psychological research to enhance work performance, select employee, improve product design, and enhance usability.

- Developmental Psychology - This specialist area is the branch of psychology that looks at human growth and development over the lifespan. Theories often focus on the development of cognitive abilities, morality, social functioning, identity, and other life areas.

- School Psychology - This specialist area is the branch of psychology that works within the educational system to help children with emotional, social, and academic issues.

- Biological Psychology - This approach is the only area of accessible psychology that studies how biological processes influence the mind and behaviour.

Ironically though; Biological Psychology will never be rolled out unless you've been through surgery, a crash or a smash. Yet this approach is the only area of accessible psychology that studies how biological processes influence the mind and behaviour. Now there's no getting away from it *Biological Psychology* is still light years away from where it should be by now but at least it's sort of heading in the right direction. The only problem is as ever when undergoing medical interventions, your future will depend entirely upon the training of the psychologist responsible for driving any biological investigations. You may well find that in most instances he or she just simply reverts back to or refers you to another Clinical Psychologist on the grounds of costs or insufficient evidence to warrant extensive testing.

I have a magnificent body that supports me in all my endeavours

Throughout my darkest days I battled like a Spartan albeit a very ill Spartan to find the root cause of my illness and I was frequently told by medical representatives, 'no we're not testing you for this or for that'. Or 'we can't keep on testing for different things indefinitely Mr. Hardy you're simply going to have to understand that you have a psychiatric problem'.

Now there is absolutely no doubt that if we feel low it's difficult for us to feel happy until we shift our mind set. We see that day after day in the emotions and moods of ourselves and our kith and kin. It's simply preposterous to suggest to someone who is ill that if they change their mindset things somehow will resolve and they will feel better.

You see; life as we know is not like that, we are not like that, there are always impositions placed upon our bodies which make it impossible for us to feel happy simply as and when we choose to feel happy. The best we can ever hope to do is to recognise and accept that we have a part to play in that process yet understand that we do not always hold all the keys. So the question remains, is 'psychological illness real or simply a medical form of illness fiction?'

Well there's no doubt in my mind that there are many forms of psychological illness, but in the absence of firm biological data I cannot accept or agree that psychological illness is an illness in its own right. If the root course of a problem cannot be qualified then it MUST fall into the category of symptoms from an unknown disease. Therein there must be a concerted effort made to search out the origin of that disease and not simply to attempt to treat the symptoms with dangerous views, perceptions or drugs. Under no circumstance can an unknown disease be morally written off as an emotional or psychological illness because I would respectfully suggest that act in itself constitutes gross clinical malpractice.

At the point I began to understand my realities I knew my life would change

I therefore advocate that anyone being written off by a medical representative, must document that incident via a formal communiqué to their practice in readiness for future legal action. It is only at the point we start bringing the medical industry to account, day after day that we will:

- Get the services we so desperately need.

And

- Weed out the 'luddites, rogues and charlatans' who shouldn't be in the industry in the first place.

I have a magnificent body that supports me in all my endeavours

The global market place we live and work in is full of medics desperately looking to explore new boundaries. So if we don't have the quality home grown medics that we need who are prepared to accept that we're all part of the 21st century. Then I say, lets simply offload the; 'luddites, rogues and charlatans' to the unemployed wastelands where they belong and lets import brighter, fresher service support professionals as we would do with plumbers, builders, electricians and engineers.

You see; as a former sufferer of all that's wrong with our insidiously flawed medical model we simply don't have the time, money or resolve to bring the luddite bastions of our medical industry kicking and screaming into line with our modern needs, standards and expectations.

We need effective medical services now, not light years from now, but tomorrow, or at the very latest the early part of next week. What's more we can all play our part in bringing about change; help create a medical model that is technically competent, robust and able to meet ALL our needs. Start today, and let's hope that no one ever has to document the level of personal suffering that I've been forced to document and voice via *Raphael's Legacy* etc.

At the point I began to understand my realities I knew my life would change

Exploring lymes disease pragmatically

Exploration Six

I have a magnificent body that supports me in all my endeavours

At the point I began to understand my realities I knew my life would change

Be scared, be very scared if you live in the Scottish Highlands, the Lake District, the Yorkshire moors, the New Forest, The Welsh Hills, The Peak District, The Cotswold's, Dartmoor or any British town or village. For there is a disease so deadly out there it can literally destroy your life in a matter of days not weeks! But this disease is not one that you've probably ever been warned about; because this is a disease that our government and our chief medical officers refuse to accept is a major problem or even here amongst us today. So deadly is this disease that it can be spread through sex, through food, through the placenta, through ticks, through midges, through mosquitoes and through wild animals and domesticated pets that have fleas. The disease that I refer to is no other than the life sapping, body destroying, Lymes Disease or its official name the Borrelia burgdorferi Bb spirochete. Typical Lymes Disease symptoms include:

1. Sudden unexplained skin rashes with a whitish centre.
2. Joint pain.
3. Joint swelling.
4. Stiff neck.
5. Unexplainable fatigue.
6. Flu-like symptoms.

I have a magnificent body that supports me in all my endeavours

7. Frequent fevers and shivers.
8. Frequent sore throat.
9. Heart irregularities.
10. Depression & mood swings.
11. Digestion and stomach related problems.
12. Difficulty eating nausea or vomiting.
13. Muscle twitching or muscle cramps.
14. Indications of sinus infection.
15. Hypoglycemia.
16. Bell's palsy.
17. Carpal tunnel syndrome.
18. Vision problems.
19. No mobility in muscles or tendons.
20. Sensitivity to light and sound.
21. Cranial pain or symptom of pressure inside head.
22. Strange shivers up and down spine.
23. Dizziness unsteady on feet.
24. Seizures unexplained blackouts.

Typical Associated Neurological Problems include;

1. Manic–depression.
2. Short-term memory loss.
3. Poor concentration.
4. Slow mental processing.
5. Brain fog.
6. Sleep disturbances.
7. Hallucinations.

At the point I began to understand my realities I knew my life would change

Lymes Disease the great pretender can also mimic;

1. Multiple sclerosis.
2. Anorexia nervosa.
3. Alzheimer's disease.
4. Parkinson's disease.
5. Bipolar depression & psychosis.
6. Hypothyroidism.
7. Fibromyalgia.
8. Guillain–Barré syndrome.
9. Cranial nerve disturbances.
10. Heart abnormalities.
11. Arthritis.
12. Gulf War syndrome.
13. Obsessive compulsive disorder (OCD).
14. Attention-deficit/hyperactivity disorder (ADHD).
15. Chronic fatigue and immune dysfunction syndrome (CFIDS).

Now I'm not going to dwell or delve too heavily into all the issues associated with Lymes Disease. But is important that we as a society sit up and tack notice of the fact that when we have a condition in our midst that is not responding to treatment, it is vitally important that we test patients for Lymes Disease. The reason being that I believe that bloody disease is wrecking too many lives is simply because its potential presence is not being considered or detected and instead people are just being fobbed off by clueless medics with diagnosis such as; ME, CFS, Depression, Stress, etc, etc, etc.

I have a magnificent body that supports me in all my endeavours

The difficulty however that we all face if we are infected with this disease is that there is a lot of misreporting about this disease, where common dictum suggests that:

(a) It doesn't exist in the UK.

And

(b) If you do contact it which is highly unlikely or so the medical world would say, it can be cured with a few short weeks of antibiotics.

Both those statements are completely wrong, it is here and you can be infected very easily and as yet there is no effective one stop or fully ratified treatment process through to cure.

On top of that diagnosing Lymes Disease can be a very difficult task, which is why so many cases are missed, or patients are diagnosed with other illnesses entirely.

You will acquire no support from the NHS in your endeavours to be either tested or treated for this disease and so it's very important to note that if you believe you have this condition you must take the initiative and privately fund your own investigations.

However please note that whilst there are a number of laboratories used to try to detect Lyme Disease the vast majority are notoriously inaccurate, often producing "false negative" results, i.e. showing that a patient does not have Lyme Disease when in fact they do and I can certainly relate to that.

At the point I began to understand my realities I knew my life would change

Way back in 1988 I tried to engage my GP with the spectre of Lymes and was immediately poo poo'd by him. So I went out and had the wrong lymes test performed privately *which cost me a lot of money at the time* and it came back negative. The very fact that it came back negatively threw my chances of recovery completely off line for a further 17years whereupon in desperation I had the correct form of the test performed resulting in the confirmation of ballistic levels of lymes.

So why are there so many false negatives? Well the reason for this is due to the fact that the Borrelia burgdorferi spirochete is so adept at evading both our immune cells and conventional bacterial detection methods. In laymen's terms it's just too darn difficult to be detected by the protection processes in our body and by normal clinical processes used to detect disease. Borrelia burgdorferi, does not have one single, static appearance or chemical signature, and is able to alter these in order to evade detection. In this way, Borrelia burgdorferi is therefore able to evade standard laboratory testing procedures and when you add the fact that there are over 250 known strains of Bb, it becomes obvious that this truly is one very elusive bacterium.

I have a magnificent body that supports me in all my endeavours

It is not uncommon therefore for a patient to be highly infected by Lymes Disease only to repeatedly produce negative lab test results. You can see how these poor souls just like I was; get tarnished and written off by the medical world as neurotic and hence offloaded to the shit which is psychological and psychiatric intervention treatment regimes and zero treatment options designed specifically to address any underlying diseased states e.g. Lymes Disease. So then how are you going to make sure that if you have Bb that you:

(a) Identify it correctly?

And

(b) You identify it with the degree of speed you need?

Because

(c) It's important to note that every week wasted can add literally months onto the painful task of clearing this dreadful disease from your body.

Well you're going to have to either engage your clinical practice in the first instance or find some qualified person who can extract blood from you. You're then going have to contact the Bowen Research & Training Institute in North America and request their Bowen Q-RiBb test vials and transfer packaging etc. The term Q-RiBb stands for, Quantitative Rapid Identification of Borrelia Burgdorferi which is a relatively new test was developed by Jo Anne Whitaker, M.D. an international medical researcher and a Lymes disease patient herself. The method uses a fluorescent antibody technique on whole blood. As it is 'quantative' the test can determine the extent of infection and that is precisely why I

At the point I began to understand my realities I knew my life would change

chose the test for myself. A preliminary report of the findings is provided to the patient within 24 hours of receiving their blood specimen and final report including digital photographs is issued a few days later. Now that's what I believe medical investigations should be all about i.e. rapid testing and rapid reporting coming together as one. The other great thing about this test is that the Q-RiBb is the only test that is unaffected by whether the patient is currently or recently has been taking antibiotics. The reason that is important is because as previously mentioned Bb can detect when it's under threat and can change its form or identity via masking hence evading all other screening processes. It cannot evade however this screening method, so if you do have lymes this test will prove it.

Let's take this situation one step further now, let's assume that you have had your results and you have tested negative for lymes via Q-RiBb, what do you do? Well you do all that you can do to find out what's really wrong with you because that's all anyone of us can ever do. Assuming that you agree with me that laying down and doing nothing is simply no way to live or be. You see I personally dislike names and handles that are thrown out and anchored onto patients by the medical industry e.g. she has OCD, he has ME, she has MS, he has IBS, he has Lymes Disease etc. There is far too much of this and not enough help for patients with these terrible conditions. The unfortunate truth however is that we can either choose to live with those handles and use then as our crutch or we can battle and fight for a better quality of life. In the greater schemes of things it doesn't matter which sits most comfortably with us because as individuals in our own right we each have the right to choose which path we'll follow in life and it really is as simple as that.

I have a magnificent body that supports me in all my endeavours

Now if your tests are negative and you still choose to battle for a better quality of life then there is a stark reality that you're going to have to wise up to. You're never going to get the sort of help and support that you need from our fundamentally flawed NHS. I know its annoying that a terrorist bomber can get a blood transfusion to save his or her life and that a paedophile can have his coronary bypass performed regardless of the former suffering he's caused during his life. But that is the way of things and I know that it simply doesn't make sense that those 'deviants' can get what they want when they need it and yet no one either hears the suffering or pain of those amongst us infected with Lymes Disease. But that is precisely why we need detach completely from the hypocrisy of those who cite the Hippocratic Oath in order to moralize the actions they take.

By accepting and not allowing ourselves to get hung up on the way things truly are we actually empower ourselves. With that shift in perceptions we're able to accept that the NHS always fails the chronically ill and because of that we can never be let down by it ever again. It is only at the point that we begin to recover that we can begin to kick and scream out loud that our so called glorious NHS is nothing but a cash hungry dinosaur filled with brains the size of peas. But don't despair there is help out there and there are solutions to insurmountable problems to be found. All we need to do is be careful yet willing to explore the potential of alternative views on disease, the treatment of disease and our perception of living and life.

At the point I began to understand my realities I knew my life would change

As a working class lad who fought tooth and nail for the NHS I never ever would have thought I would find myself saying that money is the only thing in clinical care that can move you out of the darkness and into the light. But if you are ill and wish to recover, I'm saying it loud and clear right now, you will need to read, to spend your own money and then spend and read some more.

There are no magic wands, no miracles or benevolent healers at hand; chronic illness recovery starts only when a proper diagnosis has been made and an effective treatment process undertaken. At that point and that point only can your unnecessary suffering start moving towards an end.

Nevertheless I always say this to anyone suffering from a chronic illness if you're not making any progress on the treatment regime that you're on, you've either had the wrong diagnosis or your treatment protocol is wrong. The only reason I can say that is because as you will read in the later chapter The Treatment Explorer, I've got a wardrobe full of treatment failure t-shirts.

However I'm not the sort of guy who will stick with a treatment if I feel it's false or an untruth; because my fervent belief is that for a return to health there must be a point when we finally get over the chronically ill pain and suffering hump. And if that isn't happening then the treatment isn't working and it's time to understand:

- Why not.

And

- What you need to do to move that situation on.

I have a magnificent body that supports me in all my endeavours

There are many diseases out there responsible for chronic illness, some apparently treatable some not, all I can say is if I'd bought into the rubbish that I'd been sold for years, I wouldn't be writing this book now because I would never have made any form of recovery.

Nevertheless I've covered a Bb test result coming back negative, but what happens when it comes back positive. Well sadly it's not much different from above, you won't get the sort of help you need from the NHS. You're going to have to:

- Apply a multi pronged approach to ridding your body of as much of it as you can, including the neurotoxin load that it has produced.

- You're going to have to get you endocrine system working well again as well as your liver to ensure that you're able to remove the remnants of this disease from your body.

- Above all you're going to have to be strong, because the journey through to recovery is both difficult and possibly lifelong.

At the point I began to understand my realities I knew my life would change

EXPLORING GENETIC TIME BOMB LINKS PRAGMATICALLY

Exploration Seven

I have a magnificent body that supports me in all my endeavours

At the point I began to understand my realities I knew my life would change

Whilst I've explored conditions, perceptions and diseased states from a highly personalised view point and position in this book. I nevertheless believe that my pragmatic views originate from nothing more than an enquiring mind, stimulated by great personal suffering and learning. I have no great gifts to bring to the world, no great deeds to accomplish; save to try to acquire some grace and peace in this life for myself and to be brutally honest it really doesn't get any more complicated than that. You see; I personally don't believe, having suffered far too much that there is any great majesty in suffering. I believe as an evolved society we should have gotten through most of our unnecessary suffering by now. Yet if there is anything rewarding about chronic illness and suffering it is that we have time to revisit things that we once took for granted. In doing so, we afford ourselves the opportunity to explore our life and backgrounds from newer and more informed perspectives.

During the process towards my own personal recovery I looked at my mum, her background, her health conditions and the imposition that may have placed upon me. Not really what you would can an implicitly abstract case but certainly one that allowed me to shed more light upon her and the impact that genetics can have upon us all.

I have a magnificent body that supports me in all my endeavours

My mum I'm informed was an extremely vivacious yet devout Roman Catholic, who had a zest for life complemented with a strong moral undercurrent. She loved people, animals, the outdoors and her favourite rugby team Whitehaven RLFC. She would frequently cycle hundreds of miles with her friends when not at work and help her dad in the garden taking much of his manual work. In fact nothing was a problem to her until she was struck down by two major illnesses in very quick succession. At 15 she was struck down by rheumatic fever only to sort of recover before being knocked for six at 16 with scarlet fever. My granddad, over the years I knew him, would frequently in his broad west Cumbrian dialect state, *'duz thou no marra, thee mother our Nancy was niver sham lass efter she ed scarlet end rumatic fever'*. He was indeed right, because from that point on:

- She would get tearful over silly things.

- She frequently had low moods.

- She would get tired quickly.

- She could sleep for England.

- Her thought processes were often confused.

- She was always cold.

- She always had pains in her joints.

At the point I began to understand my realities I knew my life would change

By the time I was born and after much stress and much heartache my mum was already being treated with antidepressants and she'd already been written off as a nutter by her own family and my dad's callous and intolerant extended family. I spent all my childhood years removing and emptying buckets of urine from my parents' bedroom as my mum refused to leave her bed. Making her meals etc, and many, many times simply battling with her in floods of tears as I tried my level best to prevent her from committing or attempting to commit suicide whilst:

- My brother watched TV downstairs.

- My sister was in bed.

And more importantly whilst

- My dad simply lost himself in his horse racing or 4 pints of beer in kells legion or the red lion pub.

Such a life, such personal experiences at a tender age can be difficult to reconcile as we mature and I guess that's why I began doing so much work on myself at a very early stage in my life. The thing is, its only now that I've been through what I've been through that I'm able to totally forgive myself for any anger I had towards my childhood as well as any anger I had towards my mum for the dreadful childhood we had. I can't excuse either my brother or my father for their reluctance to engage or even to attempt to help or support my mum, but in reality I don't feel that I need to, they made their choices, that's just the way they are. It is however clear to me now that my mum has suffered greatly from social and clinical prejudices for the majority of her life.

I have a magnificent body that supports me in all my endeavours

She's been through hell, medications, had electrodes placed on her head, injections, psychiatric incarcerations, operations and physical and emotional suffering beyond belief. But to her testament she's still with us in 2008, alive and kicking for all her might, a colossus in terms of those who have alienated her, insulated her and ridiculed her for a lifetime of undiagnosed suffering and pain.

It's only now that I understand that she never ever recovered from rheumatic or scarlet fever, that her body was constantly in a toxic state, that her detoxing capabilities and her ability to cope were as impoverished as her finances and her limited joys in life. It's actually very upsetting now to understand just what she was forced to endure and also very annoying that this should have been imposed upon my mum. All of her suffering and years of waste through nothing more than sheer medical ignorance and the sociological prejudices of her kith and kin.

Now the reason that I've covered my mum's predicament is because I believe that it's eminently possible that our health can be compromised at any time in our lives by a raft of unseen genetic time bombs. I refer of course to placenta transferred neurotoxins and low grade disease states; I refer to industrial chemicals and toxins trapped in our DNA. I refer to genetically damaged biological process systems and organs all of which constitute a variable and a ticking time bomb in our ultimate physiological state of wellbeing. Now the previous postulation is not as abstract, challenging or as ridiculous as it would first appear. You see in days of yore man discovered that if he planted his weakest fruits of the harvest, his harvest the following year was a disaster. However when he planted his finest fruits his harvest the year after that had vitality and there was food in abundance. In essence he was proving that vitality propagates vitality, whereas disease propagates deformity and living matter with a reduced vitality.

At the point I began to understand my realities I knew my life would change

Well we as individuals in our own right are nothing more than the products of our parent's fruits, a product of their vitality or paradoxically a product of their diseased states and a myriad of other things. There has been some research on this matter specifically focusing upon the impact of holocaust experiences upon the lineage of survivors. But whilst results have concluded that biological systems have been impaired in the majority of instances, no global acceptance of hereditary impositions via such roots has been forthcoming as yet. A position I would suggest is more to do with medical prejudices and historical perceptions than it has to do with due consideration and clinical expressions of acceptable probabilities. But then again we know that the medical industry is the last remaining bastion of, antagonistic, for the sake of it and protectionist luddite men.

Unfortunately however, research into the imposition of historical toxic lifestyles, the industrial revolution, chemical warfare, chemical manufacturing and disease is negligible. Yet we know that all those variables killed our forefathers with impunity but not before their fruits were sown with other such contaminated souls in the creation of whole new generations. For instance, my modern industrial contamination lineage consists of coal mining, steel making, mustard gassing, textile manufacture, nuclear generation / reprocessing and chemical manufacture to name but a few. Now there is no way that you can convince me that the toxic cocktails that my family worked in, breathed in or were impregnated with before eventually killing them is not in some way playing a significant part in my life story. Simply because it's impossible for them not to be that's why I believe we need to stop simply living in the moment and start building smarter profiles when we become, because that's the only way we're ever going to get the full picture and put the stabbing in the dark approach to bed finally and for good.

I have a magnificent body that supports me in all my endeavours

We know so little about the complexities of DNA toxic transfers, but we know that excess exposure to radiation and many forms of toxins be that, poisoning in low or high dosage, does effect and can damage a host's DNA. We know this because people die from such impositions it's as simple as that. Our DNA is nothing more than a blueprint from its previous owners and if their DNA was damaged, why shouldn't ours be equally damaged and prone to very subtle levels of developmental, repair and replication discrepancies which manifest at any point in our lives as subtle disease states?

I will take that one stage further. What if subtle issues with our DNA don't actually present themselves as a disease state later in life? But actually contribute to new disease states simply because the impositions placed upon our bodily functions, due to impediments in our DNA, render them weaker or less able to deal with the issues they're presented with. What if 'Barry Hardy' was born with historical mitochondria conjugates, which meant that my body's ability to detox at a cellular level was significantly compromised prior to point zero? Why then shouldn't I go on to develop serious and chronic health conditions? No matter what my body tries to do to fight off disease invaders, it's simply unable to offload the by-products of that battle and therein my body becomes toxic.

I hope you see where I'm coming from here, we all must have encountered chesty friends at school, kids who's summers were a nightmare due to hay fever etc, but neither us or they truly knew the origins of such impositions. Equally until we ourselves are presented with a health challenge we naturally believe that we were born healthy and that we've just sort of picked up a disease later in life. But my point is, unless we explore all avenues, all reasonable lines of research we have no idea what sorts of ticking time bombs lay deep within us. Because of that we may

At the point I began to understand my realities I knew my life would change

never truly understand what it is that we really need to do to return us back to some form of quality of life once we've been struck down by a chronic illness.

I'm therefore advocating that lineage must be considered when exploring possible imposition sources to our health issues, but word of mouth and subjectivity in the detection process are simply not good enough.

We need to test and look for clues, for markers and for answers, because deep within us may just be the key that we've been looking for. That must be our starting point to recovery, the point we've prayed so hard for and I say that with all seriousness because I advocate that the legacy of more ignorant times may indeed still be wreaking havoc with the life forces trying to live in so called, more enlightened times.

To fully appreciate what I'm saying here we need to stop biologically living in the moment, we need to stop making snap shot biological value judgments, we need to accept and appreciate that we are the products of yesterday's men and women. We live in bodies that are nothing more than receptacles of historical DNA, the very same DNA that was malnourished and poisoned, generation, after generation, after generation. So the next time you get angry about the imposition your health places upon you, stop your thought process right there and take the time to connect with:

- Who you really are.

- What you really are.

And

I have a magnificent body that supports me in all my endeavours

- The suffering that your DNA experienced long before it manifested itself as you.

Simply because

- Your body may only be trying its best to deal with the fall-out imposed upon it by the historical damage imposed upon your historical DNA.

On a more personal note if there's any spark of delight I take from the formulation of this chapter it's that I realise and I'm fully content with the fact now that; with no birth children to my DNA my DNA and all that it is, is effectively over at the point I take my last breath…….yay.

Perhaps part of my battle to refine my Raphael Treatment Protocol (RTP) was nothing more than to arrive at that point, who knows, and furthermore, who save for me, really cares because in truth it was only my life path to walk anyway.

At the point I began to understand my realities I knew my life would change

A Personal Closure

People often remark about the beauty of birth and then fail wholesale for a whole host of reasons to rejoice daily in the beauty of any given substance of birth. Similarly those very same people seem compelled to shy away from for the absoluteness that is our mortal passing, feeling it inappropriate to either discuss or explore the very essence of mortality. I've never had those problems, for I've always endeavoured to rejoice in the beauty of all the products of birth and am blessed enough to see our mortal finality as nothing more than blessed release from the pain we've endured for so long.

There is absolutely no sadness for me when a souls time is finally up, for I simply thank it and them for all that he, she, they were and for all that he, she, they aspired to be. At that point there is something deep inside me that allows me to let him, her, and them go to the place where their energy at that point needs to go and/or be. So I've shed very few tears over a blessed departure from mortality during my life, for I know that they all spent their time amongst us well and for that I feel nothing but unquestionable pride and admiration of and for them including the major part they played in my life.

I have a magnificent body that supports me in all my endeavours

It's important to note here that whilst I do not and never will shy away from the rigors of mortality, I'm tormented by its love, its finality and the great loss that it inevitably brings to us all. My belief is that when we connect in mortality we certainly learn to grow, but after that growth spurt we are often left with far too much time to reflect and participate in self flagellation based upon highly preventable regrets. That is I suspect one of the many frailties that we all encounter in being simply a mortal, maybe that's a life challenge that we all as mortals need to accept or at least try to conquer, but when all said and done who amongst us truly knows?

At the point I began to understand my realities I knew my life would change

EXPLORING PHYSIOLOGICAL STRESS PRAGMATICALLY

Exploration Eight

I have a magnificent body that supports me in all my endeavours

At the point I began to understand my realities I knew my life would change

Stress appears to be simply everywhere, every time you talk to someone they tell you how stressed they're feeling, stressed about work, the wife, the husband, the girlfriend, the boyfriend, the kids, their finances and so on. 'Stress' seems to be an everyday part of life. Stress; what a great word if you're a medic, you can write so many things off as being stress related. 'You're suffering from stress Mr. Hardy'

- *Patient*: 'Blimey am I? That sounds dreadful is it treatable?'

- *Medic*: 'Hmmn well it depends upon what you mean by treatable'

- *Patient*: 'Shit, tell me, what is this stress when it's at home then because it sounds a bit serious?'

- *Medic*: 'Hmmn well that's the $60.000.00 question isn't it?'

- *Patient*: 'Er…. is it? Okay let me ask you then the $60.000.00 question, what is stress?'

- *Medic*: 'Hmmn, well you see Mr. Hardy no one actually knows what stress is'.

I have a magnificent body that supports me in all my endeavours

- **Patient**: 'Er….. sorry no one actually knows what stress is and yet you're telling me I've got it, you're having a bloody laugh mate aren't you? How on earth can you say I have something when no one knows what the hell it is?'

The medic at that point then loads his or her Mr, Mrs or Ms. Pompous, Nasty or Arrogant head on:

- **Medic**: 'Look just take it from me Mr. Hardy, you're suffering from stress and I should know because I've seen it so many times in people like you!'

So let me ask, how many of you have encountered that line of clap trap? How many of you have spoken to or consulted a so called expert about a stress related issue and found that you've never been given a straight answer? That there was an undercurrent postulated that perhaps your personality was somehow contributing and even generating its manifestation.

At the point I began to understand my realities I knew my life would change

Yet the funny thing is its so simple to define stress, it really is, so are you ready for this? If so, then take a deep breath, relax and prepare yourself to be suitably unimpressed. Stress is the generic name used to identify the physical and emotional symptoms of adrenal fatigue or in worse case scenarios adrenal burnout. Got that? It sort of roles of the keyboard so I'm going to type that little ditty again, *Stress is the generic name used to identify the physical and emotional symptoms of adrenal fatigue or in worse case scenarios adrenal burnout.* That's right, you haven't got some terrible and incurable disease, you're not insane, you haven't had a nervous breakdown and you're not a neurotic waste of space.

You're normal; you're a potentially fully functioning mortal who unfortunately for some reason is experiencing the very real and terribly debilitating symptoms of adrenal fatigue or in worse case scenarios, adrenal burnout. Stress is, and be under no grandiose illusion nothing more than that. It is an eminently recoverable issue with your adrenals and that is it in a nut shell.

Phew that was an easy chapter to put together eh? We've qualified what stress is so I guess I can move onto my next chapter? Hmmmn if dealing with stress was as simple as understanding its root cause how simple life would be, but life is not simple at all! You see; I've sold you a line of thought about the root cause of stress, but now I need to qualify what on earth the adrenals are or you're none the wiser.

The adrenals are just two little walnut sized organs that sit on top of our kidneys on either side. They are responsible for producing a whole host of lovely life giving hormones not least of which include: Adrenaline, DHEA and Cortisol. Now don't worry if this sounds confusing or too technical because to help simplify the myth of stress generation I've knocked up some sketches to explain the issues I'm about to cover.

I have a magnificent body that supports me in all my endeavours

So what am I talking about when I refer to the adrenals? Well I'm referring to two critical organs within the endocrine system. 'Blimey' I can hear you say, 'what on earth is the endocrine system? This is starting to get difficult to follow'. Well just hang on and don't worry, the muddy water will clear very soon; just go with me for now yeah, because the endocrine system is just an aspect of our central nervous system. Our adrenals job is to perform a vital aspect of our nervous system. When we are in a state of adrenal fatigue or burnout and our adrenals are unable to perform well this is often the point where ignorant medics colloquially describe your presenting condition as nothing more than, 'stress or 'you've had a nervous breakdown'. Out will come the SSRI's and you will be written off without any further investigations.

At the point I began to understand my realities I knew my life would change

However for anyone wishing to recover from nervous system fatigue or burnout it's important to understand just what the nervous system is. You see, our nervous system is basically made up of two major systems, the sympathetic and the parasympathetic nervous systems which are commonly called the autonomic nervous system. These systems work in balance with each other and directly or indirectly affect almost every structure in our body including our: heart rate, blood pressure, lumbar function, kidneys, blood vessels, stomach and intestines. The parasympathetic aspect of our autonomic nervous system has mainly a relaxing function whereas the sympathetic aspect is the key to our successful survival as far back in days of yore i.e. when we needed the ability to cope in a world when everything either wanted to eat, shag or kill us. Our autonomic nervous system is most important in two situations: emergency situations that cause fear and require us to 'fight' or take 'flight' *sympathetic*, and none emergency situations that allow us to 'rest' and 'digest' *parasympathetic*. Our autonomic nervous system also acts in 'normal' situations to maintain normal internal functions and works with the somatic nervous system i.e. the systems which allow us to relax and sleep.

'Hang on, hang on, stop right there, I can hear you say, where is this going there's been lots of words about lots of things and yet the adrenal stress thing hasn't been mentioned yet'. Relax yeah, all in good time, you'll fire up your sympathetic nervous system if you're not careful and then you'll get yourself too agitated to read on. If that were to happen you won't want to finish this explanation just as it's getting to the most interesting and eye opening part for you. So in order to keep you onboard I'm going to move this on quickly now.

I have a magnificent body that supports me in all my endeavours

Let's put you in a stressful situation and let's see what happens to you? Well actually let's not because you don't need the hassle. Okay so let me make it easier; let me tell you what happens to you when you're in a stressful situation. Well what happens is that immediately your body's sympathetic nervous system kicks in and reacts in time old fashion to signals it's receiving from your thoughts about the potential danger you feel you're in.

You immediately get the fluttering butterflies in your stomach and start to feel a bit panicky; the bronchial tubes in your lungs widen to give you more oxygen so you start to hyperventilate and may even become light headed. Also blood is sent in greater volumes to your brain whilst your skin and internal organs get less and that sort of unnerves you. Your body's muscles tighten up around the shoulders, neck and your head and your heart meanwhile feels as if it's in your mouth, but your mouth feels parched.

Did I miss anything? Er…. no I don't think so unless you're also one of the many that also experiences a need to evacuate your bowel or bladder or both together when you're feeling a little stressed!

Okay, that my friend is normal stress reactions covered, and that my friend is something that was once a very close companion of mine. But let's not call it stress from now on lets call it what it really is: 'endocrine hyperactivity and or adrenal insufficiency'. It's not a mental health issue; it's not a personal weakness, but a real physiological condition which can push us all beyond our own personal points of mortal endurance.

At the point I began to understand my realities I knew my life would change

Now it's sort of easy to understand why this condition has been ignored by the medical world and sort of dropped wholesale in the mental health world. This is because its symptoms can have profound emotional implications and what's more, mainstream endocrinologists don't accept grey areas of disease such as subtle insufficiency. More importantly as I've discussed already, mainstream medicine is simply happy to treat symptoms and is therefore not in the least bit interested or concerned about identifying the underlying cause of a condition. However whilst I can understand the historical incompetence's that generated this situation, I'm simply not prepared to accept this approach and appalling level of technical expertise from highly paid public sector workers in the 21st century because its quite simply an outrageous situation.

So I'm going to explain adrenal insufficiency to you now in I hope an engaging and simplistic fashion, but before I do that I would like to have a look at the two sketches I did way back in 2003 when trying to understand what was happening to me. I deliberately haven't updated them, save for giving them a title because I wanted you to try to connect with where I was then. They are as raw today as the day I put them together and yet when I put them together in my desperate state, absolutely no one said to me, 'Yes I see now Baz what you've just described makes sense I've got it, what you're actually suffering from is adrenal insufficiency mate'.

I have a magnificent body that supports me in all my endeavours

No what I got was clap trap and rubbish, what I got were responses like these:

- 'Well he must be bipolar if he can do things like that whilst depressed and claiming to be stressed'

Or

- 'He can't be that depressed or he wouldn't be able to do things like that'

Or

- 'He's obviously just an attention seeking neurotic'

I also got a lot of mental health crap, I got a lot of:

- 'Sort yourself out crap'
- 'Why don't you just connect with nature crap'
- 'Hey I really can't be bothered with you mate crap'

Anyway, enough already, just have a look at the next two flow diagrams and see if you can relate to them and then I will begin to break down the adrenal insufficiency mystery for you, bit by bit……

At the point I began to understand my realities I knew my life would change

Manic Depression At Close Quarters

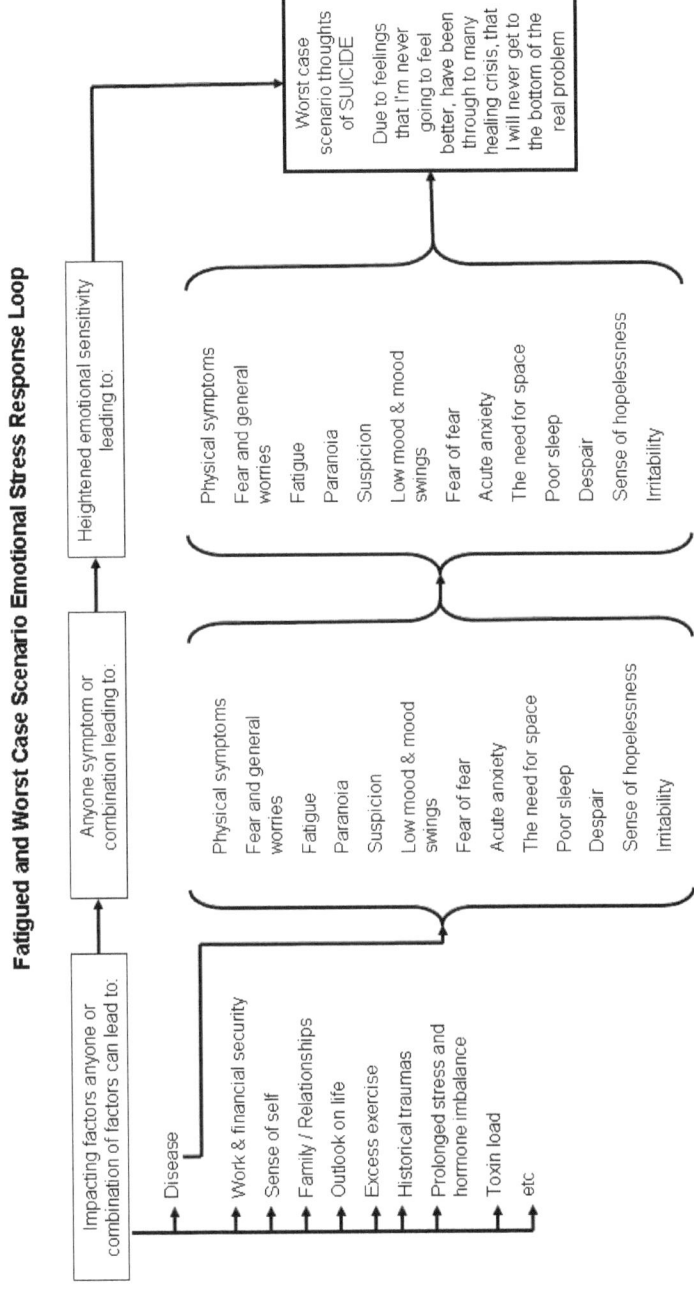

I have a magnificent body that supports me in all my endeavours

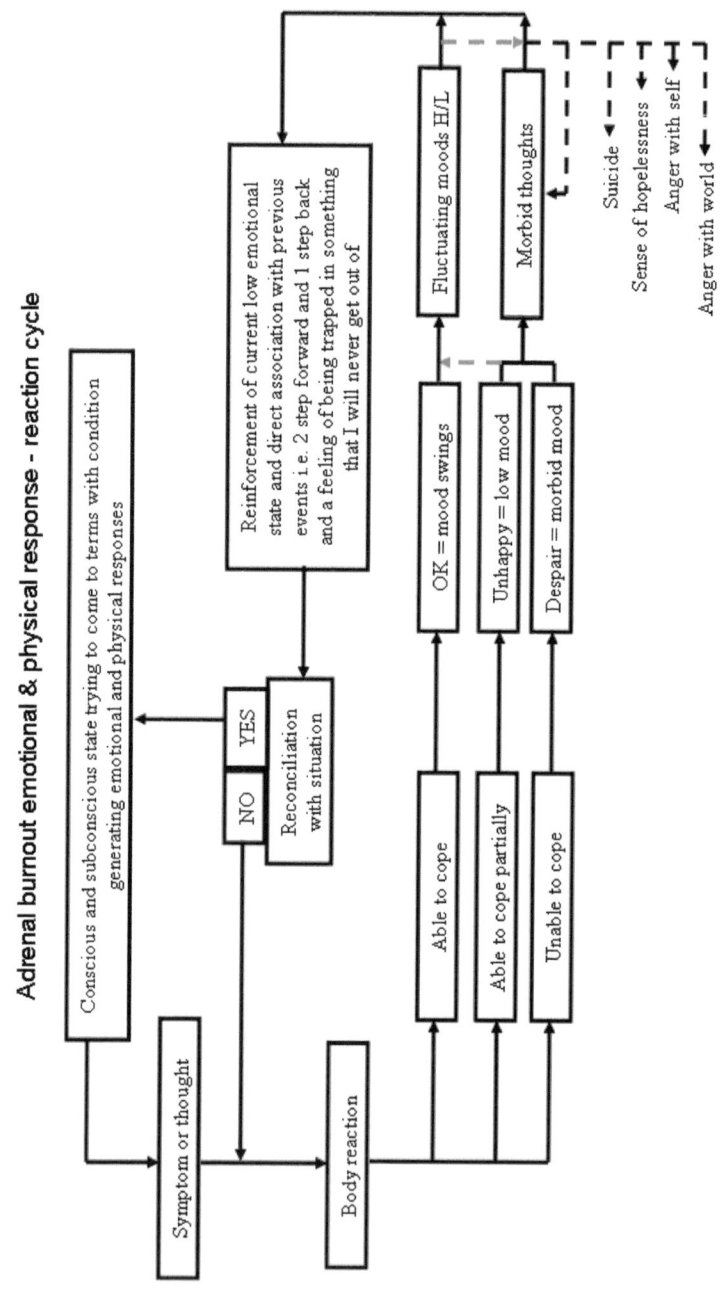

At the point I began to understand my realities I knew my life would change

So why was I experiencing such terrible and life debilitating symptoms when suffering from adrenal insufficiency? Well to understand that we must first explore the endocrine system, its major components and what they do inside our body.

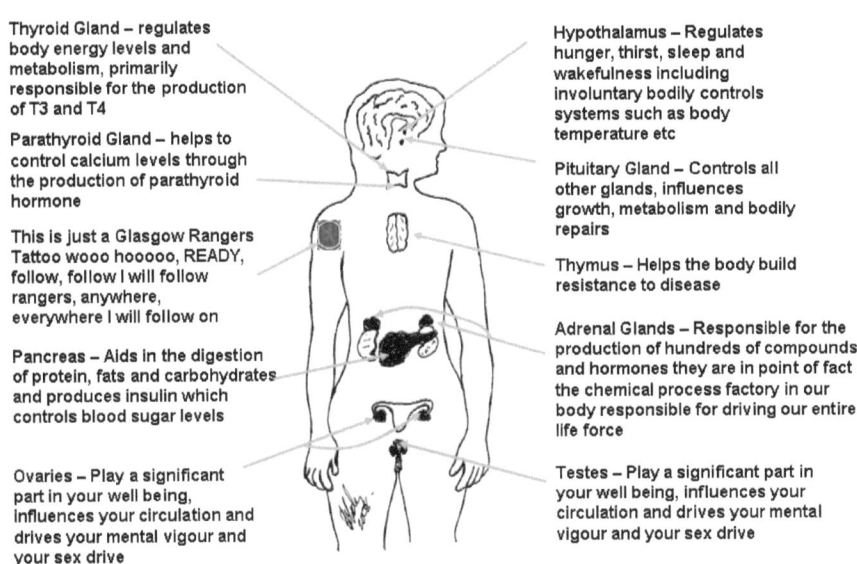

Your Endocrine System Simplified

Thyroid Gland – regulates body energy levels and metabolism, primarily responsible for the production of T3 and T4

Parathyroid Gland – helps to control calcium levels through the production of parathyroid hormone

This is just a Glasgow Rangers Tattoo wooo hooooo, READY, follow, follow I will follow rangers, anywhere, everywhere I will follow on

Pancreas – Aids in the digestion of protein, fats and carbohydrates and produces insulin which controls blood sugar levels

Ovaries – Play a significant part in your well being, influences your circulation and drives your mental vigour and your sex drive

Hypothalamus – Regulates hunger, thirst, sleep and wakefulness including involuntary bodily controls systems such as body temperature etc

Pituitary Gland – Controls all other glands, influences growth, metabolism and bodily repairs

Thymus – Helps the body build resistance to disease

Adrenal Glands – Responsible for the production of hundreds of compounds and hormones they are in point of fact the chemical process factory in our body responsible for driving our entire life force

Testes – Play a significant part in your well being, influences your circulation and drives your mental vigour and your sex drive

Is a man responsible for all his thoughts or is he at the mercy of his body? - Your choice

As you can see, the endocrine system in our bodies is simply a series of organs. However, what you can't see yet is that within those organs there is a hierarchy of process initiators and inhibitors via feedback loops within the body. To me there is no difference between that process and any modern manufacturing situation i.e. when things are right the process runs smoothly and the results are good, when things are not right the process does not run smoothly and the results are not so good.

I have a magnificent body that supports me in all my endeavours

All we need to do to is connect with that reality and to substitute results that are good for 'happy' and results that are not so good for 'depression'. So as discussed earlier when our endocrine or autonomic nervous system is running normally, five main things happen in our body via our sympathetic nervous system when we're scared, in danger or feeling threatened.

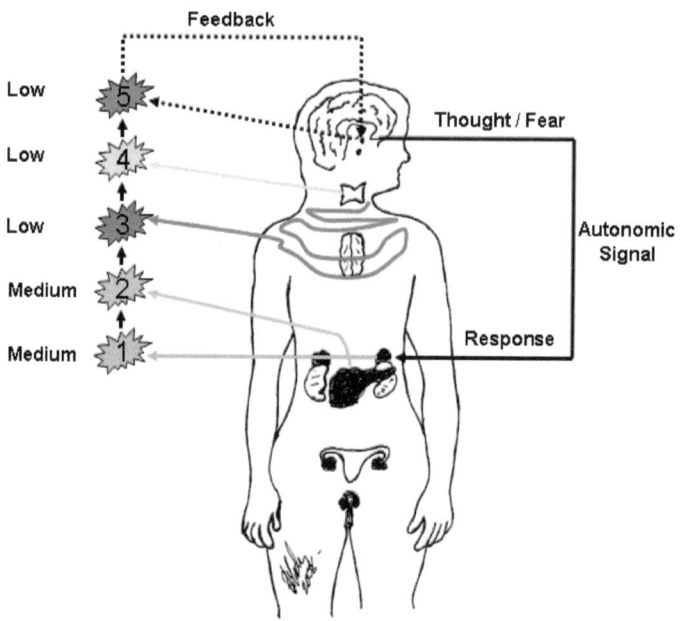

**Is a man responsible for all his thoughts or is he at the mercy of his body? –
Your choice**

An incident happens which shocks or threatens us; a boo, a car horn or a bumpy flight, it doesn't really matter. At the point the shock hits, a message is sent from your hypothalamus to your adrenals and they immediately pump out low volume adrenaline, that's the butter fly sensation you feel in your stomach. Now if you remember, I said that our autonomic system is still primed to work like it did way back in days of yore when it was at the forefront of our ultimate survival capabilities, i.e.

At the point I began to understand my realities I knew my life would change

something is going to eat me, shag me, kill me, I need to get away etc. Our adrenalines primary function is to propel us clear of danger i.e. 'flight'. Shortly after the adrenaline surge has hit, it is shut off and cortisol is pumped from the adrenals. Cortisol is a fantastic substance; it is the staff of life, without cortisol we simply die. It is cortisol that gives us the courage to turn and fight, to get out of bed in the morning, to recover from illness, it is in essence, the elixir of life, the only hormone that allows man to adapt and cope with anything. Sounds too good to be true, er…..not really, it is fantastic stuff, but as with anything too much of it is no good for anyone.

So that's biological response one (1) taken care of and its reactive level is medium in a healthy body. At the point cortisol is released, a message is sent to the pancreas which encourages it to release insulin into the blood stream. That's to also energise the body and it is also a medium response in a healthy body. So we now have response two (2) covered yeah? The body's muscles begin to tighten in preparation for activity and in a healthy body that's a low response and covers biological response number three (3). Response number four (4) then kicks in and it too is low, it's the thyroid producing T3 and T4 hormones to support and energise our metabolic rate. The danger may have simply passed by now and we think via response number five (5), 'bloody hell or phew'. Then continue along as normal not giving the incident much thought.

In essence our body then simply settles down and we're able to continue business as normal, working, gardening, relaxing, reading, watching the TV etc. We know that we are in a healthy state when this very normal bodily function takes place and it has absolutely no impact upon us or indeed our overall quality of life. When we move into a diseased state however it is I'm afraid to say a very different proposition, our quality of life falls, our sense of self is diminished and our moods are

I have a magnificent body that supports me in all my endeavours

frequently turbulent to say the least. We can quickly move into endocrine hyperactively when our body is under attack, which results in insufficiency and more often than not we begin to experience symptoms of depression expression.

We Are Always Off Colour When We Move Into A Diseased State!

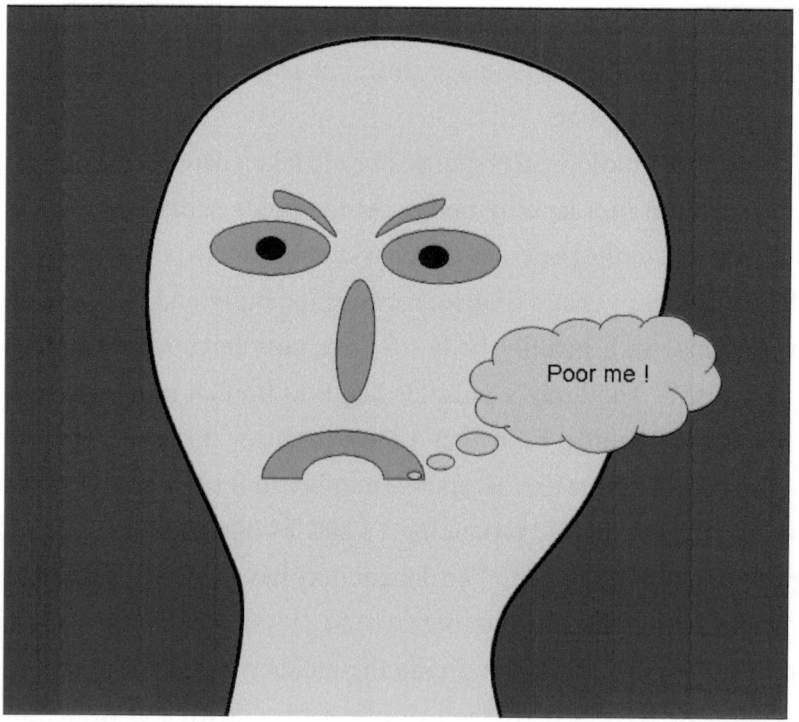

Take a very good look at this face, the colour of this face and the expression it carries with such pain, being stressed out of your body and mind is no joke at all and not in the least bit served well by luddite medic's who can only prescribe SSRI's or mental health act incarcerations.

At the point I began to understand my realities I knew my life would change

When we move into a diseased state or are moving into adrenal fatigue, our responses, whilst following the same pattern, taken on considerably different magnitudes. Values in our 1 to 5 biological responses change and we find that: *Response 1* now results in 'higher 'amounts of adrenalin and cortisol being pumped out. *Response 2* now results in 'medium' amounts of insulin but this may oscillate between 'medium and high' levels of insulin being pumped out which can push us into a, 'Hypoglycemic state' *Response 3* now results in 'medium' muscle tension, it may stay longer or it may be more noticeable. *Response 4* now results in 'great' demands being exerted upon the thyroid and as such it may not be able to meet all the demands placed upon it, changes to body temperature occur and unexplainable pains. *Response 5* now results in 'conscious awareness' of the problem and we start to become preoccupied with the condition.

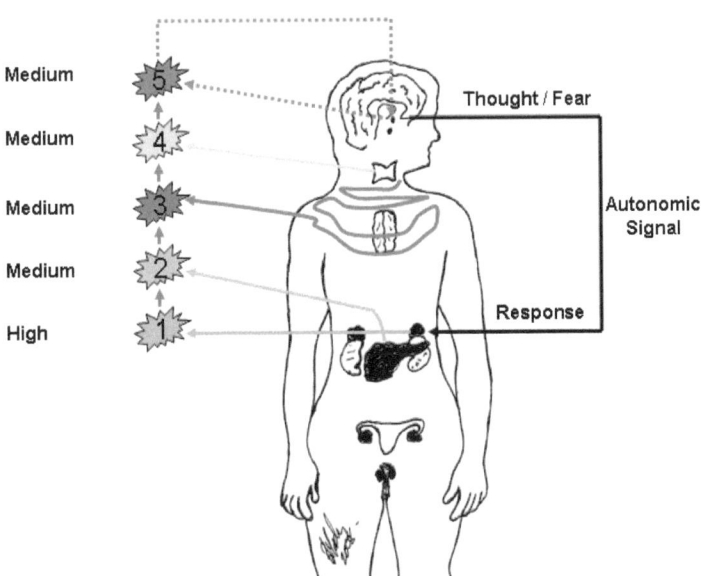

Is a man responsible for all his thoughts or is he at the mercy of his body? –
Your choice

I have a magnificent body that supports me in all my endeavours

It's important that I cover Hypoglycemia at this point because its presentation can have very profound effects upon our quality of life and sense of well being. People who suffer from 'glycaemia' related conditions can either be hypoglycemic or hyperglycemic. When we move into a hypoglycemic state we can suffer from a number of serious symptoms including comas etc. The best way to minimise these symptoms is to follow a straight forward hypoglycemic diet. A hypoglycemic person should avoid sugary foods & never miss a meal if possible. If you do miss a meal this can make blood sugar levels decrease and so symptoms will start and all this puts an every increasing strain upon your endocrine system. The best solution for a hypoglycemic is to have a personalized diet which will ensure your blood sugar levels are kept at the right levels and serious symptoms can be avoided. This is not a cure for Hypoglycemia it is merely a necessary addendum to help you optimize your health by lowering the physical stress expression being imposed upon your compromised endocrine system. Symptoms of Hypoglycemia include:

- Being constantly hungry or tired.

- Highly irritable for no good reason?

- Feeling depressed even though you have no obvious reason to feel down?

- Suffering from insomnia, where you often lay awake night after night unable to get your racing mind to calm down.

- Feeling as if you're a slave to the constant cravings you have for potato chips, soft drinks and sweets.

At the point I began to understand my realities I knew my life would change

When we move into a 'deeper' diseased state or we move towards adrenal burnout, our responses, whilst following the same pattern, taken on considerably different magnitudes. Values in 1 to 5 biological responses change and we find that: *Response 1* now results in 'high' amounts of adrenalin and 'low' amounts of cortisol being pumped out and so the fear factor increases but our ability to cope reduces significantly. *Response 2* now results in dramatic oscillation between 'medium and high levels' of insulin being pumped out and we find ourselves in a constant hypoglycemic state. *Response 3* now results in 'high' muscle tension; it may be a permanent impediment causing tension headaches, stiff neck and lack of mobility in general. *Response 4* now results in 'dramatic' demands being exerted upon the thyroid and the thyroid may move into a hypothyroid state simply unable to produce the hormones we need to regulate our body metabolism. *Response 5* now results in a vulnerable, depressed, anxious and confused state with racing thoughts, and we think we've gone insane.

I have a magnificent body that supports me in all my endeavours

It is generally at this point that we force ourselves to either see a GP or an alternative practitioner because living in our body is becoming a very difficult proposition to deal with. Only those who have ever experienced this appalling physical situation truly understand the sheer torment that mortality can be. It is a dire situation simply lacking in any rationale where your body can completely eclipse all your former beliefs and sense of who you are, as it pushes you beyond your own personal levels of endurance. It's the point where you're possibly written of as a neurotic, a depressive or simply someone with a weak psychology, when in reality you're merely in a state of adrenal insufficiency.

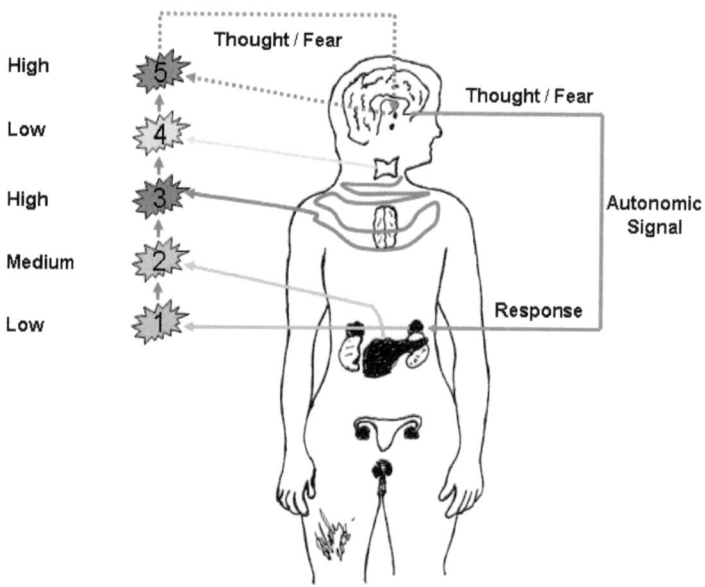

Your Endocrine Burn Out Cycle Simplified

**Is a man responsible for all his thoughts or is he at the mercy of his body? –
Your choice**

At the point I began to understand my realities I knew my life would change

Now I'm going to use that stupid 'kop out' word again, I'm going to use the word, 'stress' and why am I using it? Well because I want you to digest what I've been postulating. Then I would like you to decide for yourself if you have 'stress' or you have an expression of, 'endocrine hyperactivity or adrenal insufficiency'. With 'stress' you have an incurable enigma, with an expression of 'endocrine hyperactivity or adrenal insufficiency' you have an insight into perhaps what's going on in your body. If you agree that you could have 'endocrine hyperactivity or adrenal insufficiency' then give yourself a big hug. Because you've reached a point where you can begin the process of self ownership of the problem and a significant improvement in your quality of life is possible.

If you disagree with what I've just postulated, then give yourself a big hug also for being strong enough to live by your own beliefs and I wish you well on your forward journey. But please STOP READING this chapter and book right now it's simply not for you, but hey that's cool!

However if you're interested in moving into better health than turn to the next page but please do spare a kind thought for all of those readers you now leave behind.

I have a magnificent body that supports me in all my endeavours

Assuming that you've concluded that you do have some form of 'endocrine hyperactivity or adrenal insufficiency, then relax and above all don't get too excited. There are many many issues that can cause those symptoms and just thinking you have the problem simply isn't good enough. You need to test, to test and then test again as I outline in my chapter on, Depression, you see you don't have any condition unless you can prove it. There are so many things that move you into a endocrine hyperactivity or adrenal insufficiency and you will make no recovery by just treating those systems. You need to find out why you've moved into that state and treat according to disease findings, not symptom expression.

Now that situation is slightly complicated as I've already discussed because the medical world is simply not interested in root cause analysis. There is also the other major problem when experiencing endocrine hyperactivity or adrenal insufficiency, the medical world only recognises three endocrine conditions, Healthy, Cushing Disease and Addison's Disease. So if you start approaching medics about endocrine hyperactivity or adrenal insufficiency you will be simply ridiculed.

But why would you be ridiculed by the medical world over endocrine hyperactivity or adrenal insufficiency? Well because endocrinologists and mainstream medics only understand excess cortisol and very low cortisol; they simply do not accept endocrine hyperactivity or adrenal insufficiency as a real physical problem.

At the point I began to understand my realities I knew my life would change

So what is high cortisol? Is that what you may experience in adrenal fatigue? Er…no it's not actually. In medical terms excess cortisol is classified as Cushing's disease. This is a hormonal disorder caused by a non-cancerous pituitary tumor that produces large amounts of adrenocorticotropin (ACTH) for an extended period. The excess ACTH causes the body to produce extra cortisol, the symptoms of which include excessive weight gain, fatigue, and purplish stretch marks on the abdomen, thighs, and breasts.

So why would my high cortisol levels not be detected? Well it would be like comparing the height of mount Everest with Skidaw in the lake district, both are very high mountains but they are as different in height as chalk and cheese are in texture.

Okay but surely my low levels of cortisol in the burn out stage would be picked up? Er…..no they wouldn't I'm afraid! Low level cortisol is where the body has stopped producing cortisol completely and so it's not a case of cortisol being low as in adrenal insufficiency it's a case of there being no cortisol at all and in that situation Addison's disease is diagnosed. That is an illness in which the adrenal glands stop producing hormones that are important for certain bodily functions. The most common cause of Addison's disease is an autoimmune disease. Other causes of Addison's disease include tuberculosis and chronic infection. Common symptoms of Addison's disease include chronic fatigue, muscle weakness, and loss of appetite. Addison's disease, though incurable, is a condition that can be treated and controlled with medication.

I have a magnificent body that supports me in all my endeavours

'Hang on, hang on I can here you say that's precisely what I have, why am I not diagnosed with Addison's disease and treated'? Well the answer is very few people are ever treated for this condition; you really do need to be at death's door before this condition is treated seriously and even then patients are frequently messed around with poor medication and poor clinical management of their condition. This is so depressing isn't it? How do decent people with serious issues stemming from an endocrine hyperactivity or adrenal insufficiency issue move forward?

Well the answer is, they privately fund a twenty four hour saliva stress index profile, which is able to determine precisely where their adrenal function really is. If your adrenals are functioning well, than your circadian rhythm should be normal, i.e. your cortisol levels should be in keeping with normal circadian rhythm expectations as indicated on the first graph on the next but one page. Normal circadian rhythm consists of rising levels of cortisol from midnight until 'six am' where it should hold for an hour or so. This is essential because it is this rise in cortisol that enables us to get out of bed and cope with whatever the day has to offer. Our cortisol levels continue to fall during the rest of the day until by 'ten pm' our cortisol levels should have reached their lowest production levels. This reduction in cortisol level reduces autonomic stimuli and therefore allows us to relax and sleep.

You can see a dramatic change in cortisol production levels when the endocrine system is in an abnormal state with the red line in the second graph running much flatter but higher than normal levels, indicating high levels of cortisol. The green line running much flatter and lower than normal levels indicating low levels of cortisol production. But what do these changes mean? Well because our adrenals are responsible for so many diverse functions, their fall into an abnormal state has profound effects upon our body and sense of wellbeing.

At the point I began to understand my realities I knew my life would change

When excess cortisol is present we may feel wired, unable to relax, paranoid, angry depressed and unable to sleep because of racing thoughts and whilst this lack of sleep causes fatigue, we're simply unable to knock our body off to enable us to sleep no matter what we try. That's why people in this state often turn to drugs and alcohol etc, as a means of escape, but the reality is that in pursuing that route further complications arise.

Conversely when low levels of cortisol are present, we're unable to cope, we may have a heightened sense of anxiety and depression due to high levels of DHEA, but equally we maybe fatigued beyond endurance because we're simply too tired to relax, cope or sleep. Experiencing endocrine hyperactivity or adrenal insufficiency is a very challenging experience but let me be brutally honest, no amount of reflexology, SSRI's, happy clappy thoughts of higher things will alleviate its symptom matic expression. Why you may ask? Well because those simplistic approaches are nothing more than like flapping your hands and expecting to fly. Anyone who tells you anything different to that is a complete charlatan and business sales, self motivated, compulsive liar.

I have a magnificent body that supports me in all my endeavours

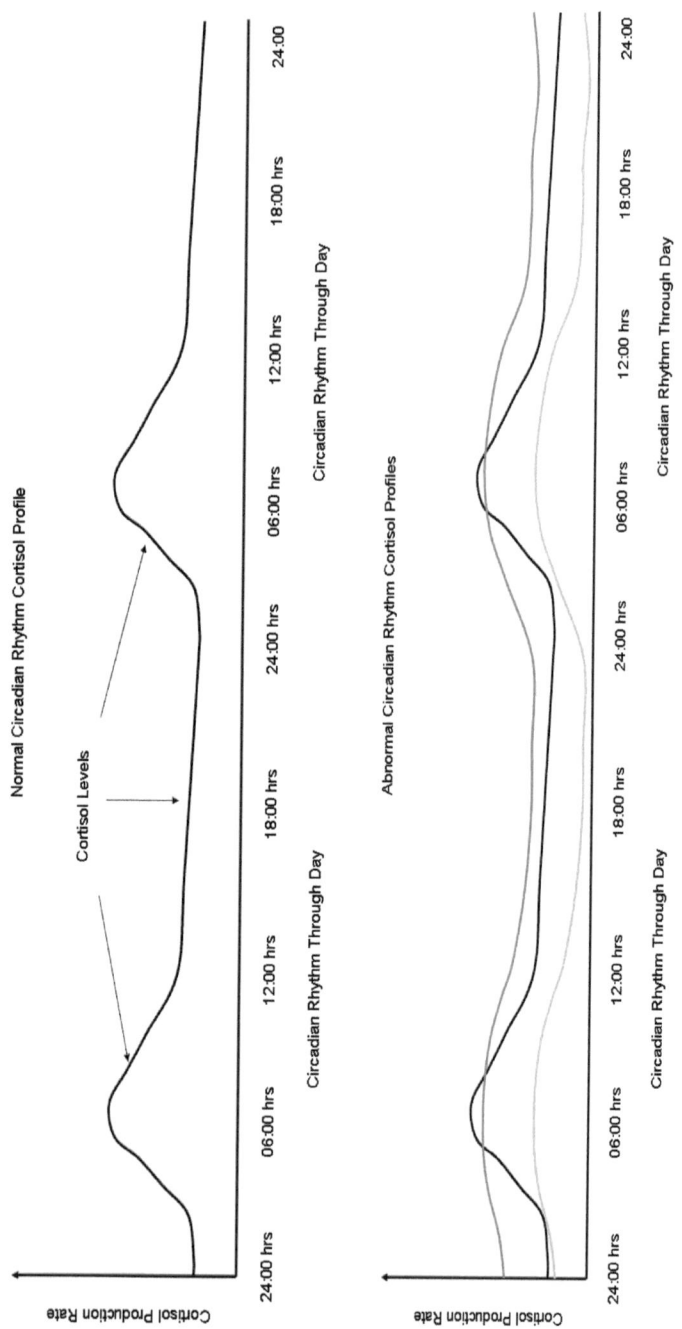

At the point I began to understand my realities I knew my life would change

Now I can just hear you screaming, 'enough already, just what do I do to recover from this condition? Well I'm afraid there are no quick fixes, and furthermore the process of recovery can be challenging because there are so many contributory factors to be considered however your starting point must be:

1. A shift in perceptions to enable you to understand precisely what's happening to you and to your body.

2. Testing to find the root cause of your conditions.

3. Putting a holistic treatment protocol in place designed to help you recover and to help you with that process, I've developed my recover mapping approach, which is on the next page.

I have a magnificent body that supports me in all my endeavours

Staying in control of your situation requires nothing more than a structured approach to what you're trying to achieve.

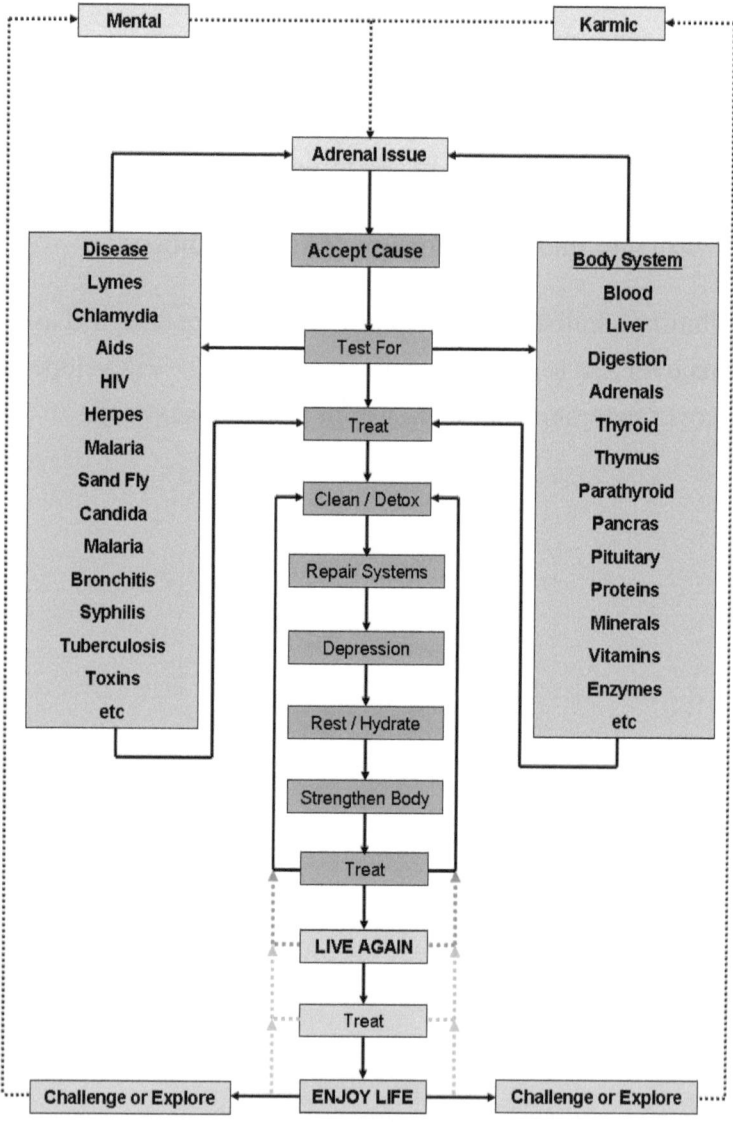

Does a man move into a faulty adrenal expression because of the state of his mind or is he pushed into that expression because of the state of his body? – **YOUR CHOICE !**

At the point I began to understand my realities I knew my life would change

Manic Depression At Close Quarters 115

Let me re-cap on what our sympathetic and the parasympathetic nervous systems are in relation to bodily support functions.

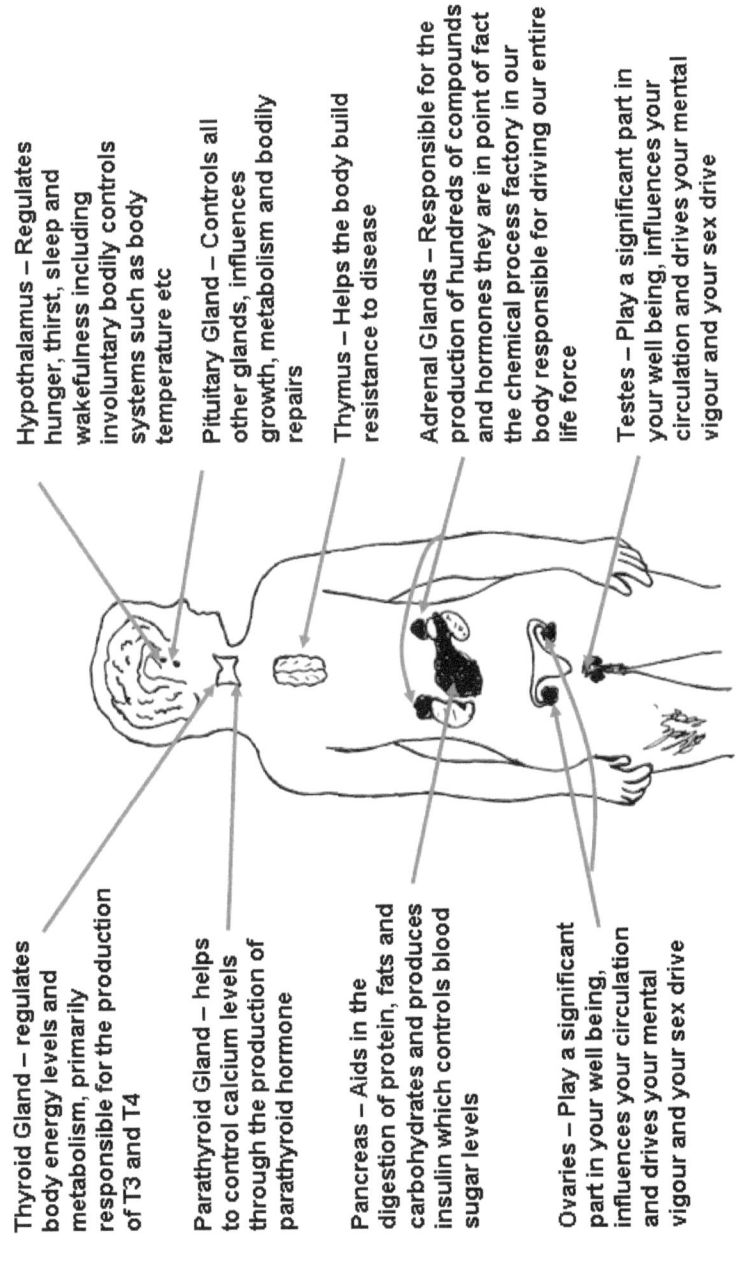

Your Endocrine System Simplified

Hypothalamus – Regulates hunger, thirst, sleep and wakefulness including involuntary bodily controls systems such as body temperature etc

Pituitary Gland – Controls all other glands, influences growth, metabolism and bodily repairs

Thymus – Helps the body build resistance to disease

Adrenal Glands – Responsible for the production of hundreds of compounds and hormones they are in point of fact the chemical process factory in our body responsible for driving our entire life force

Testes – Play a significant part in your well being, influences your circulation and drives your mental vigour and your sex drive

Thyroid Gland – regulates body energy levels and metabolism, primarily responsible for the production of T3 and T4

Parathyroid Gland – helps to control calcium levels through the production of parathyroid hormone

Pancreas – Aids in the digestion of protein, fats and carbohydrates and produces insulin which controls blood sugar levels

Ovaries – Play a significant part in your well being, influences your circulation and drives your mental vigour and your sex drive

Is a man responsible for all his thoughts or is he at the mercy of his body? - Your choice

I have a magnificent body that supports me in all my endeavours

At the point I began to understand my realities I knew my life would change

EXPLORING DEPRESSION EXPRESSION PRAGMATICALLY

Exploration Nine

I have a magnificent body that supports me in all my endeavours

At the point I began to understand my realities I knew my life would change

Clinical depression is defined as a state of intense sadness, accompanied with the absence of pleasure or the ability to experience pleasure. Unfortunately many people mistakenly identify the feeling of being depressed as 'feeling sad for no reason' or 'having no motivation to do anything'. But clinical depression is more serious than normal depressed feelings, because it often leads to constant negative thinking and thoughts of escapism through either substance abuse or through self harm. It is precisely because of this populist misunderstanding, ignorance and society's intolerance of this disease that individuals suffering from this condition find themselves with nowhere to go. The most common feelings associated with clinical depression include:

- Feelings of overwhelming sadness and/or fear.

- Changing appetite and marked weight gain or loss.

- Disturbed sleep patterns, such as insomnia.

- Fatigue, mental or physical, also loss of energy.

- Feelings of guilt, hopelessness, loneliness and anxiety.

I have a magnificent body that supports me in all my endeavours

- Trouble concentrating, keeping focus or making any form of decision.

- Recurrent suicidal thoughts or plans for committing suicide.

Despite depression being a simply appalling condition it's still regarded by society as a personal weakness. General perceptions are that it's not a diseased state but that it's something that weak people use to highlight their weakness. Therefore because it's not regarded as a diseased state those suffering from it are therefore not given the level of support or assistance that individuals with lesser but clearly more visible conditions get.

But why isn't this condition regarded as a disease? Well because the medical world has failed wholesale for millenniums to bottom out the root course of this condition. It doesn't matter whether a sufferer sees a GP, a psychologist, a psychiatrist, a counsellor, a herbalist, or a homeopath etc, it's always the same result. The symptoms are the primary point of interest and then the patient's background becomes the main focal point. All parties have different approaches, orthodox clinicians go for the soft options of sedation and detachment whereas alternatives clinicians attempt in the majority of instances to fight fire with fire taking the depressive condition head on.

Neither of those approaches work in the majority of instances because they don't actually try to determine what is really wrong with the patient. To me and having been through what I've been forced to endure, it's simply ridiculous that detailed testing is never carried out but completely understandable because:

At the point I began to understand my realities I knew my life would change

- Depression expression suffers from historical prejudices.

And

- Our biological and diagnostic testing techniques are frankly outrageously poor.

I have a magnificent body that supports me in all my endeavours

What the entire medical and clinical world seem to be happy to ignore is that the human body is a unit which has a multitude of direct and indirect processes working day and night just to keep our bodies in balance. Because it's much easier for them to simply write their patients off than to commit to any relevant, detailed or protracted clinical investigations.

However what happens if any one of those processes in our bodies either becomes defective or more over we are born with defective processes in the first instance? Well it's not rocket science is it? If we have defective processes we normally end up having problems and those problems nearly always present themselves as a diseased state. The impact of that can have dreadful consequences upon our lives and I cover the lifelong impact of scarlet fever and romantic fever upon my mum in the chapter Genetic Time Bombs.

Nevertheless, that's why I believe that depression expression, in the majority of instances, is not a psychological or mental health issue, it is nothing more than:

- A derivative or symptom of a diseased state.

- Placenta transferred derivatives of diseased states.

- A breakdown in generic body processes or process coding.

- Genetic abnormalities in generic body processes or process coding.

And only rarely;

- The manifestation of our perceived weak psychology.

At the point I began to understand my realities I knew my life would change

If only we were prepared as a society to accept this postulation then we would be able to accept the need to find the root biological cause of depression and not always simply write it off as an emotional or mental illness. Once a root cause is scientifically determined we are better able to treat a condition effectively and hence remove it from our lives completely.

I can hear the howls or derision right now though, 'What is this guy talking about? We always identify the root cause of depression doesn't he understand just how incredibly difficult this condition is to treat?'

Well in truth I do, you see; there were many years where I would have eaten dog shit if I thought it would make me feel better so I certainly do know how difficult living and treating depression can be.

I also know that the only reason I freed myself from that life sapping condition is because I changed my perceptions and my views upon all its possible causes. Depression, if not caused by injury to the brain, is always the result of bodily process breakdown and I mean by that the breakdown of processes within the entire body and not just the brain.

When depressed its impossible to either contemplate or attempt to simply think or rest ourselves out of depression. This diseased state doesn't simply go away of its own accord and medication which compromises still further detoxing systems in our body is absolutely no solution at all.

I have a magnificent body that supports me in all my endeavours

So what am I actually saying? Well what I'm saying is that we can't treat or medicate a condition if we don't really know what's wrong. But what we can do is shoot from the hip and think we know what's wrong and in doing so pump all sorts of shit into our body resulting in confused results at best and dangerous results at worst. That is unfortunately what happens across the board to the majority of us when we seek medical intervention for this terrible condition.

Now that's a very bold statement and what possible grounds can a plumber have to even dare to postulate such outrageous views? My answer is, nothing more than personal experience and an enquiring and problem solving mind, that's all.

You see, if we fail to enquire we fail in everything we do, because it is only through understanding the entire picture that we are able to fully understand the potential for risk and gain in anything we undertake or do.

My view is that in terms of depression treatment we've made very little progress in the past 2000 years and I believe that is purely because of our sociological attitude to this condition which is continuously preventing any evolution in our perceptions.

At the point I began to understand my realities I knew my life would change

Now I was both a civil and mechanical engineer by profession prior to having to find ways through my health conditions. Working in those professions I was exposed to many applications, many environments and many ways of being. It also became obvious to me from a very young age that in all walks of life and work there are people with, 'can do mind sets', people with 'can't do mindsets' and people who 'simply don't give a damn'. Within those mindsets there are, the conscientious and the bodgers, the well trained and the chancers, the problem solvers and the problem makers, the perfectionists and the couldn't care lessers, the owners and the off loaders. There are mind sets who try to make situations far more difficult than they really are and mind sets that inappropriately make problems lighter than they really are. That is just the way it is in engineering, in science, in medicine and in life, etc. *It is the innate paradox of man that he has the ability to be simply brilliant whilst also retaining the ability to be a complete idiot and general waste of time that never fails to blow my mind.*

I have a magnificent body that supports me in all my endeavours

But why should this paradox's have such a grave bearing upon depression? Well because at the point we buy into clubs or schools of thought or simply choose to conform we lose or chose to ignore our ability to think outside of the box. It is only the men who've chosen the hard route and thought out of the box who've have helped move all our sociological perceptions and expectations along since time began. They achieve that simply by shattering false illusions, generating new belief structures and challenging their peers to prove through science or by example that what they are saying and doing is wrong.

Now let me make it very clear here, I'm no guru, no eminently qualified man of science, I'm simply a guy with the ability to think out of the box and in that spirit I'm going to formulate a simple insight to underpin my root cause of depression views. Despite what many in the medical industry would postulate that it's impossible to draw analogies between the physical and the non physical. My considered retort is simply this; luddites why do you even aspire to work in a modern world when your minds are as closed and dark as the darkest of nights?

At the point I began to understand my realities I knew my life would change

You see; if we have an open mind it is eminently possible to draw upon the scenario crossovers that exist in all forms of science and life. Note that when I previously referred to physical I was referring to living breathing life forms and when I refer to non physicals I refer to manufactured support tools, equipment or devices. The only delineations I make between the physical and non physical are spontaneous thought, feelings and pain, barring that; everything be it physical or non physical is conceived, lives and expires' end of story.

In fact there is a simple statistical tool which describes the process of sustainability and it's called the bath tub curve. In essence, it's a graph based upon statistical data which plots predictable life profiles. It doesn't qualify pain, thought or fear it just prescriptively maps the potential for burnout, failure or death.

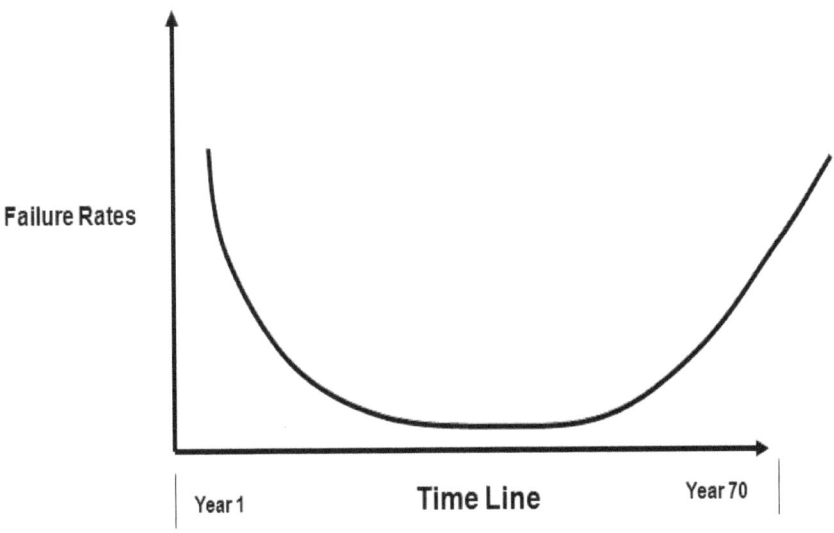

I have a magnificent body that supports me in all my endeavours

As you can see there is potential for burnout, death or failure at a very early age but that burnout, death or failure drops off until in the human case it starts to climb again at about 60 years of age. It will continue climbing thereafter exponentially as the burnout, death or failure of this standard distribution graph so reliably predicts.

Now I've used that simple thought stimulating proposal to enable me to move onto my next point, so please don't get too hung up on it, simply try to bear with me for now. You see; in all walks of life there are comparisons and crossovers that can be drawn and so if we always remain open to those potentials we can always take givens from one situation and apply them where they've never worked or been used before. Such that even when the medical world argues that you can't compare the engineering science developed by man with the biological science that some qualify as divine, I will always argue from a higher place that you can and we must do so if we are ever to improve the lot of mankind. Because the people who cry heresy are not crying heresy for any go reason at all, save to protect themselves from having to do what they're paid to do anyway.

At the point I began to understand my realities I knew my life would change

Nevertheless and moving that point on, most people are completely unaware of just how complex modern manufacturing techniques are and just how little room there is for error. All we ever see is the end product such as, the car, the watch, the sofa, the bed, the mobile phone, and the laptop etc, etc, etc. Yet these are all products of extremely complex manufacturing techniques.

Take even the simplest of manufacturing techniques; let's say for example, a chewing gum manufacturing facility or a porkpie manufacturing facility. Both require tremendous intellect and continuous intellectual investment to ensure that their product is fit for the market, meets all compliance criteria including, quality, legislative, commercial and financial investment criteria's. However in order to meet these givens in any process environment there are multitudes of process streams and because of that there is a need for a multitude of quality and compliance checks, each of which can be as easy or as complex as they need to be.

For the purpose of what I'm trying to explain, I've mapped a very simple manufacturing process with multiple process streams on the next page.

I have a magnificent body that supports me in all my endeavours

BASIC MULTIPLE PROCESS MAP

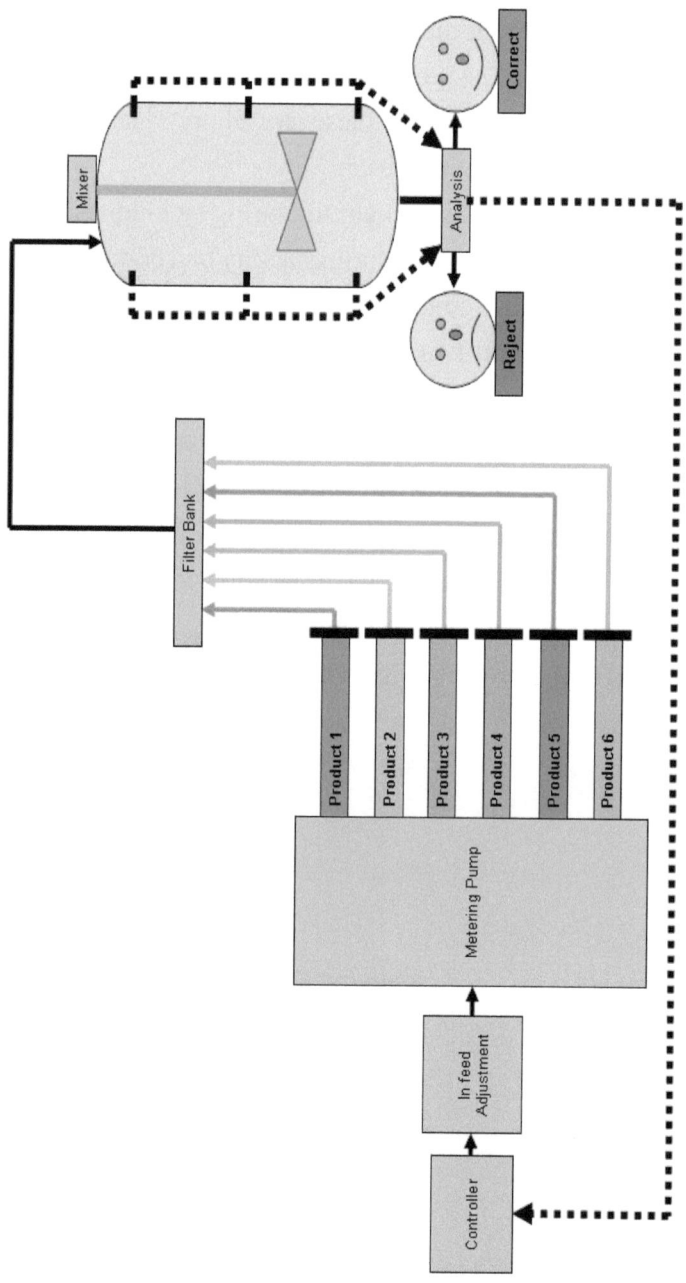

At the point I began to understand my realities I knew my life would change

You will see that my basic manufacturing process consists of:

- A logic control processor.
- Bio feedback loops back to the logic control processor.
- An in feed adjustor.
- A pumping mechanism.
- Six different product process streams.
- A filtration unit.
- An agitator or mixer.
- A main reactor vessel.
- An outlet point with analyser.
- Two final product streams correct and reject.

Now if you or I were responsible for ensuring that this simple process ran correctly, there are a few mandatory things we would need to ensure that we had in place first.

- A thorough understanding of the process and what we were expected to do and achieve.
- Robust and properly maintained support equipment and access to suitably qualified repair personnel in the event of its breakdown or failure.

I have a magnificent body that supports me in all my endeavours

- Quality compliant process streams free from contamination or degradation.

- An ability to analyse effectively when the process has drifted out of acceptable parameters and the knowledge of how to bring it back into line.

- An ability to analyse fault data and to instinctively know which part of the process was to blame.

- An ability to think logically, laterally and rationally about any and all possible eventualities as and when they arise.

Apart from those key points the only remaining holistic essentials we might require are:

- A good work ethic and a desire to do the best that we possibly can do at any given time.

Now the reason that I mapped personality profiles earlier in this chapter is that I wish now to focus upon productivity and performance.

You see, the biggest impediment we all face as a society in achieving our goals is the impact of the people factor. The people factor can either impose great impositions upon us or simply inspire us beyond belief, but it is, I'm afraid to say the greatest of all intangibles simply because when all said and done it's frequently remains outside of our control.

At the point I began to understand my realities I knew my life would change

As I've previously stated; I personally believe that anything and everything is possible when the right skills, the right people and the right approach are applied to any given problem or situation and that is the way I choose to live my life. But what matter my own personal beliefs if the people factor problem somehow keeps getting in the way as was the case with my own 30+ years of; inappropriate clinical and medical care. Nevertheless and for the purpose of discussion let's have a look at the people factor in terms of the manufacturing unit.

I have a magnificent body that supports me in all my endeavours

So the chewing gum manufacturing process has begun to drift and the product is clearly out of specification. The net result is that everything that is being produced is now being rejected. The operations lead in charge simply can't be bothered because his shift is finishing soon, so he leaves the problem to the next shift later that afternoon. The new process controller thinks, shit this problem can only be the result of a problem with process stream number three, I've had this problem before and when I increased its flow rate the process corrected itself albeit very slowly. So he cranks up process stream number three, but the product still remains widely out of spec. In reality he doesn't really know what the problem is, he's just applying at best a calculated guess at what the problem may or may not be. Well what to do next? He's worked very hard trying to sort the problem out but his shift is over soon too.

Solution, he leaves a raft of notes about what he's done, how hard he's worked and then goes onto explain what he thinks needs to be done. Shift three comes in, its late at night, the lead process controller is tired and he can't really be that bothered so he basically shuts the process down and calls in the operational manager. The operational manager goes ballistic and starts lashing out verbally at anyone and everyone in his path. He or she says 'just get this process back on I don't care what you need to do just do it and do it right now'. So the lazy shift process controller simply takes the view, sod it if that's what he/she wants I'll just fire the process up again because I'm out of here soon and it takes five hours to fire the process back up and by then I'm off shift too.

But the process won't fire up again because the product has changed completely, its solidified everywhere and now the entire process stream is blocked. The result is that the process plant now requires a major strip down and large sections of it and components from the various in-feed process streams now need to be scrapped.

At the point I began to understand my realities I knew my life would change

Believe me that is not a rare phenomenon, it's an endemic theme of manufacturing and life. When problems are not thought through correctly, when people are not fully committed or accountable then the end result is always unnecessary expenditure, trouble and strife. Or should I say unnecessary in the case of our own personal well being when engaging with representation from the medical or clinical worlds; unnecessary suffering, isolation and the real possibility of a loss of life.

Now of course it can be dangerous to think that we know all the answers, but no more dangerous I would suggest than to abstain from thinking at all. Root cause analysis, whilst sometimes painfully slow, is the only way we can make progress, because the lessons we learn frequently allow us to grow. My view is that it's just as dangerous in a manufacturing environment as it is in our own personal well being if we make value judgments based upon assumptions, prejudices whilst in an environment of fear. If we're not encouraged and rewarded to think laterally and carefully whilst remaining open to the possibility of new ideas then the end result will always be, stagnation and eventually tears because we stifle all our opportunities to grow.

Please take the time to allow these ideas to sink in and try to get a feel for my manufacturing process map. In the next section I'm going to draw some comparatives between effective and defective manufacturing and the current approaches to the analysis and treatment of depression.

I have a magnificent body that supports me in all my endeavours

For the purpose of my comparative explanation, I've mapped the same manufacturing process but I've simply replaced manufacturing terminology with biophysical terminology. You will see that the map now consists of:

- A brain not a logic control processor

- Bio feedback loops back to the brain not back to a logic control processor.

- A liver not an 'in feed' adjustor.

- A heart not a metering pump.

- Six biological substances not just six different product process streams.

- A blood brain barrier not just a filtration unit.

- An activity stimulated circulation system not just an agitator or mixer.

- A body not a main reactor vessel.

- An outlet emotional/perceptional thought process not just a set point analyser.

- Two final product streams 'happy' and 'depression' not 'correct' and 'reject'

At the point I began to understand my realities I knew my life would change

BASIC BODY PROCESS MAP

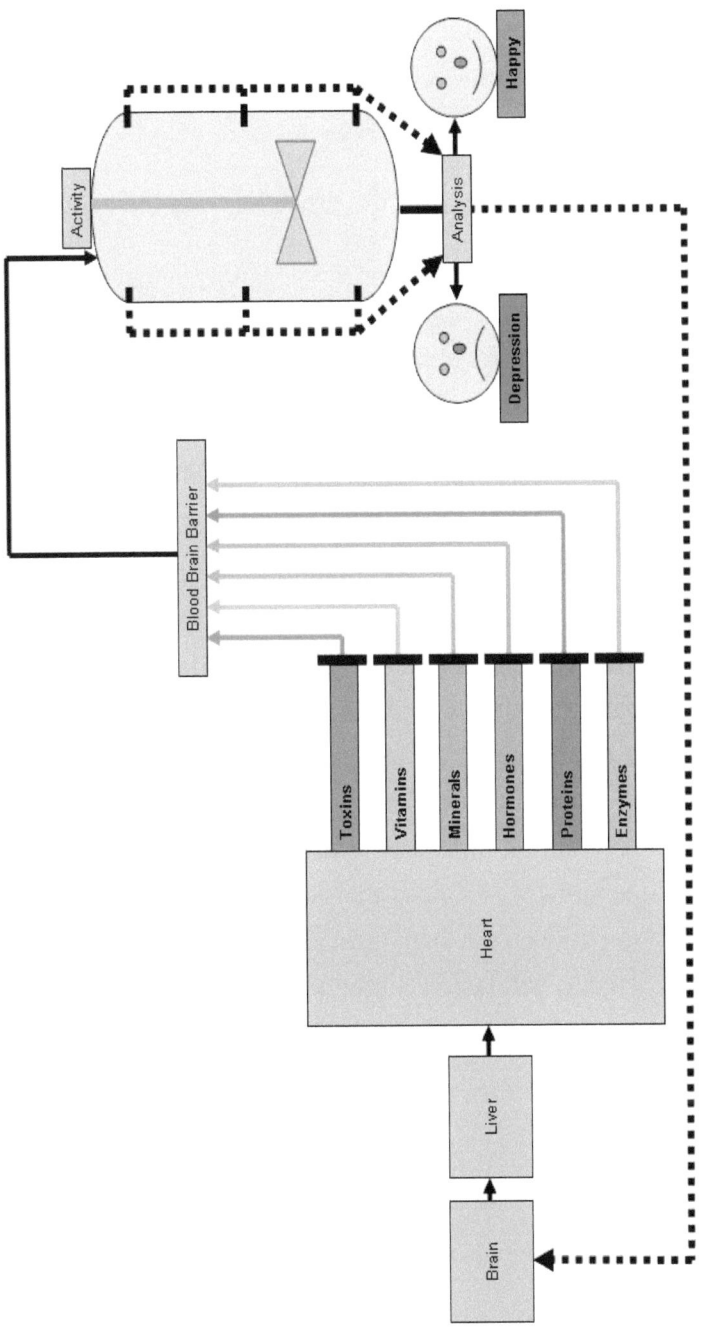

I have a magnificent body that supports me in all my endeavours

The point I'm making with the revised process map is that there is no real difference between us and an artificially created manufacturing process stream. Take out our humanistic themes and we're both nothing more than a series of complex chemical processes interacting with each other. The key in both instances is:

- How we perceive the processes and their interactions.

And

- How we are able to read the information that is generated therein.

Let's look at the first example of the manufacturing facility, clearly the fault originated from a component within the process stream and then ignorance, incompetence, bad practice, call it what you will, made that original fault much worse than it needed to be. The point I'm making is no fault can be repaired until we fully understand the root cause of that fault. In the case of the depressive state, the medic traditionally makes a snap judgment about what he/she thinks is wrong with the patient invariably without any sound clinical data e.g. symptom addressing not symptom generator addressing data.

The questions we all need to ask here are, do these so called experts understand how all our body processes hang together? And is their training restricted to out dated training in matters of the mind or are they applying holistic rationale?

At the point I began to understand my realities I knew my life would change

Well to answer those questions let's test the waters then. What happens when we present with a depressive state to a medic? Well, you may at best receive a thyroid blood test, but I will guarantee that when the results come back stating within normal values all further biological investigation will stop. You see, it doesn't matter that the criteria for that test is rubbish, which I cover later in the chapter about testing. The fact of the matter is; all further biological tests will STOP.

Now I personally don't think that snap judgments represent either effective process management or effective clinical management. In fact from a clinical perspective to me it amounts to gross clinical negligence and accompanying clinical abuse FULL STOP. Nevertheless as part of this clinical negligence and abuse loop your biological investigations will stop and thereafter you will have two choices only. Either to reject your medic's postulations or to go with his or her knee jerk treatment suggestion which in reality is based upon nothing more than:

- His or her dogma driven instincts.

- His or her reluctance to explore root cause analysis.

Or

- Hmmn I've come across this before and so here you go take these and see how you get on e.g. offered the obligatory anti-depressants.

I have a magnificent body that supports me in all my endeavours

Absolutely fine if you wish to spend a life racked with side effects and living in complete despair, but if you don't then perhaps we as individuals need to take more care. You see as far as I'm concerned the problem with taking drugs to try to fix symptoms is akin to replacing oil in our car engine with honey on a mere thought or anecdotal whim. Whilst both have similar characteristics i.e. sticky and gooey, they are in fact completely different things. But don't take my word for it ask anyone who's put oil on their toast or filled their car engine up with honey and see what sort of results they gained.

For our brains to work effectively there are a myriad of processes that must work in synergy, processes in organs, organs sending signals to other organs telling them to produce substances or equally sending signals to stop those substances from being produced. In fact we have small, dynamic manufacturing processes all over and through our body.

So let us be very clear on one thing here and that is that the process of emotional and mental well being does not simply start and finish with our brain. Our brain is merely a feeder upon the nutrients and energies that our body's in either a healthy or diseased state provide for it.

Let's look at it like this, when we go down with influenza and we feel depressed or low, are we feeling that way because we are mentally or emotionally low? Or are we experiencing the imposition of disease pressing down upon us which is making us feel mentally and emotionally low? Well I will bet that no one ever gives much thought to those two questions when they're suffering from influenza. Because in general we have the influenza and then just as quickly as we contracted it, we get over it and in time we begin to feel like our old selves. But what happens if we never feel like our old selves again after an influenza infection? Or what if from birth we've always felt like shit?

At the point I began to understand my realities I knew my life would change

Well to me the answer is very simple, we're in a chronic diseased state, a DNA or placenta transferred diseased state, an ingested or sexually transmitted disease state anyone of which could be compromising our body's ability to function as it should and so we're simply unable to feel happy, contented or good about ourselves. When systems and processes within our body are in a diseased state or their performance is being adversely affected by a state of disease how on earth can we even think that we can feel healthy or normal? The body relies upon these functions to work in synergy and if they're not in synergy then the end result is just like the manufacturing example I gave earlier, we get an indication that there is a deviation from norm. Our body will start letting us know with lots of symptoms not least of all we may become suicidal in our depression expression.

So what if we have low grade viral, fungal or bacterial impositions, what if our assimilation processes, our bodies manufacturing process break down, what then? Surely we just go to our GP's and explain what's happening to us and they simply fix us because after all that's what they're paid to do. Wrong, wrong, wrong, wrong, wrong that's what we were brought up to think in our pill popping generation, the reality is that most medics haven't got a clue about basic diseased states let alone being receptive to help you recover from one. They merely look at our symptoms like the jack of all trades that they are and *'master of none'* and put two and two together and arrive at five.

I have a magnificent body that supports me in all my endeavours

For example, if a man keeps smashing his car against the back of his garage wall every time he tries to park it, do you just put a foam buffer on the back wall? Do you fix his brakes? Do you suggest that perhaps he needs a smaller car? Or do you suggest he has his eyes tested?

Now I don't know why the guy in the last example has such a problem with parking his car, I'm simply making the point that there could be one or a whole host of reasons why he can't park his car. But the sooner he finds out the root cause of the problem the sooner he can move on. However the probability of him moving on effectively from knee jerk reactions or assumptions I would suggest is actually very low.

You see it's eminently possible that anyone of the previous parking correction suggestions could address his problem. But it's equally possible that none of them would offer any solution at all. Because we may discover some way down the line that the guy:

(a) Never passed his test?

(b) Has a wooden leg?

(c) Needs a light installed in his garage

Or

(d) Needs his hair cut?

At the point I began to understand my realities I knew my life would change

Do you get my point? Root cause analysis and only root cause analysis can possibly lift the lid on his parking problem. But one of the main reasons we don't have root cause analysis in terms of depressive expression is because the big pharmaceuticals have sold us all an illusion that they've created concoctions which actually solve that problem. The greatest proponents of this are those who've patented the familiar anti depressant classified as Selective Serotonin Reuptake Inhibitors or SSRI's. It would appear according to those manufacturers that the vast majority of depressive conditions lay firmly at the door of one single neurotransmitter which is of course Serotonin. And these drugs work by shutting some receptors down in your brain hence creating a situation where you're able to maintain artificially high levels of serotonin in the brain. So if you've got any form of depressive illness I can guarantee you that this form of medication will be imposed upon you immediately without any biological testing, because this holds the ultimate key to success in treating depression; or does it?

Well actually they don't and they don't because there are at least another five major neurotransmitters in the brain each of which play some part in our emotional expression so why is all the focus upon serotonin?

Simple of course, because the proponents of serotonin drugs have bagged and blagged the market and so what they have been postulating for years about the success rates of these drugs has now seeped into every aspect of the medical psyche and is literally perceived to be the only appropriate treatment approach when depression expression is suspected.

I have a magnificent body that supports me in all my endeavours

What happens therefore if you take these drugs? Do you feel better if your serotonin levels now increase? Well I couldn't possibly say because they never made me feel one bit better.

Instead I developed chronic nausea, headaches, fuzzy thinking, nervousness, anxiety, dizziness, low libido, significant weight gain and an immediate increase in my suicidal depression expression. Actually what I developed was an increase in **ALL** the horrible symptoms that I was actually trying to get away from. Shit you may say 'that sounds scary'. Oh yes, believe me it was very scary and very depressing excuse the pun.

You see, all I wanted was to feel much better, instead I felt much worse and in fact I felt like absolute shit. But desperate to feel some little bit better I did the rounds on these bloody things, SSRI's, NASSA, TCAs etc, etc, etc, all with the same results, no improvement but a significant personal exasperation in the resulting magnification of **ALL** the original presenting symptoms and the additional imposition of newer even more debilitating symptoms. It gets even worse however, you see; the problem with taking these substances is that:

(a) You've now become a psychiatric patient.

And

(b) You're getting further away from identifying the originating disease responsible for your condition and presenting symptoms.

At the point I began to understand my realities I knew my life would change

But that is the dilemma that the majority of people with depression find themselves in. So what is happening here? Why do people like me not get better on these drugs?

Well perhaps we never had a bloody serotonin deficiency in the first place; perhaps the neurotransmitter issue was never a major problem and our depression expression was merely a presenting response to dysfunction in other processes or the imposition of disease and disease generated toxins.

The truth is as I see it that perhaps these drugs are the best thing ever invented for some people but I've no way of judging that save from my own experiences. But just pay a visit to a depression expression forum and you'll discover that few either:

(a) Make much progress from taking them.

And

(b) The majority wish to get off them as soon as they can because of their unacceptable side effects.

However if they work for you then go for it, because I would never advocate that anyone should stop taking them if they truly want to and/or are gaining benefit from them.

I have a magnificent body that supports me in all my endeavours

Nevertheless my personal belief is in using them we're simply back to the honey and crude oil in the engine situation again. We're back to people making snap judgments about what they think will work without any substantive biological investigation results to support that judgment. In essence we're back to our chums in the process manufacturing unit and the results in that example if you remember weren't that great.

You see if our body is being attacked by things like Lymes Disease or low grade Viruses, Funguses, Chlamydia, Candida or any one of a number of genetically, placenta or socially transferred diseases, toxins or organic anomalies. Of course we're going to feel ill, low, depressed and even suicidal. Why on earth wouldn't we? Our body clearly is being prevented from performing in a fashion which allows for optimum health.

At the point I began to understand my realities I knew my life would change

It is at this point I feel the need to extinguish another insidious sociological false truth. How many times as a chronically ill person have you been told:

(a) There's nothing wrong with you.

And shortly after that being informed that:

(b) The body is a remarkable thing, always trying its best to heal and repair?

Implying that if you did have something wrong with you then your body is certainly doing its best to help you but your mind is preventing that good work happening. Well the next time anyone dares to say that to you, simply compose yourself, and look them straight in the eyes and say, 'fuck off and don't talk such bloody rubbish' If our bodies are that bloody clever, why do I feel so ill and why do mortals:

- Develop cancers which are contrary to everything the body needs?

Before;

- Eventually dying from some or all of our diseases!

I have a magnificent body that supports me in all my endeavours

Now the reason I feel so strongly about this point is because whilst I accept that the body has an abundance of program logic, I know full well that at the point our body is attacked, disrupted or compromised by a foreign logic, it responds just like a PC when attached by a worm virus. It completely loses the plot and is unable to repair itself. Those of us who've been struck down by chronic illness know precisely what it's like when everything we take either gives us a short term lift or plummets us into deeper despair. We know what it's like when our body scares the living daylights out of us every single day. We know what its like to feel that our body is constantly working against us and not for us. The plain and simple fact is that our bodily protective mechanisms in chronic illness states simply stop working completely, slow down or start producing the wrong formulas and substances which serve only to keep us in our chronic state. It is precisely those problems which prevent chronically ill people from making any real progress back to health or some degree of normality.

Yet at the point we address the underlying causes and remove toxins from our bodily systems, depression almost always becomes a thing of the past, save for low grade expression of the condition as we cleanse our body via purging over the ensuing weeks, months, years or perhaps even a life time. In a diseased state, bodily processes breakdown, incorrect volumes and expressions of chemical processes are the result. Mechanisms designed to filter and adjust flow become blocked and mechanisms designed to be selectively permeable become indiscriminately permeable. The net result of this is that we end up with a very sick body, with many differing and presenting symptoms, not least of which is an expression of depression.

At the point I began to understand my realities I knew my life would change

If the body is invaded by a disease or an impediment to normal functioning, immediately our program logic kicks in and tries to fend off that or those insults. This results in a whole host of bodily disruptions and inevitable toxins production which pushes us into a marginal toxic bodily state. But what happens if for some reason the body despite its best efforts is unable to conquer this imposition and those insults and imposition start taking over and interfering with other processes and systems causing greater confusion in the body?

What if a byproduct of this imposition is the production of high levels of toxins which cause inflammation, death and destabilization of feedback loops and organs within the bodily functions and systems. All of which are designed to regulate the production and absorption of key, wellbeing enzymes, proteins and chemicals etc!

Well the answer is simple, the body simply breaks down, damage occurs and the probability of the body being able to repair itself becomes greatly reduced. What I'm really talking about here is, toxin overload, a severely compromised liver function, a breakdown in effective bodily production and repair processes, an imposition to the body and blood brain barrier and a circulating soup which is both highly toxic and of a non standard composition and invite you to once again have a look at the bodily biophysical process map again on the next page.

I have a magnificent body that supports me in all my endeavours

BASIC BODY PROCESS MAP

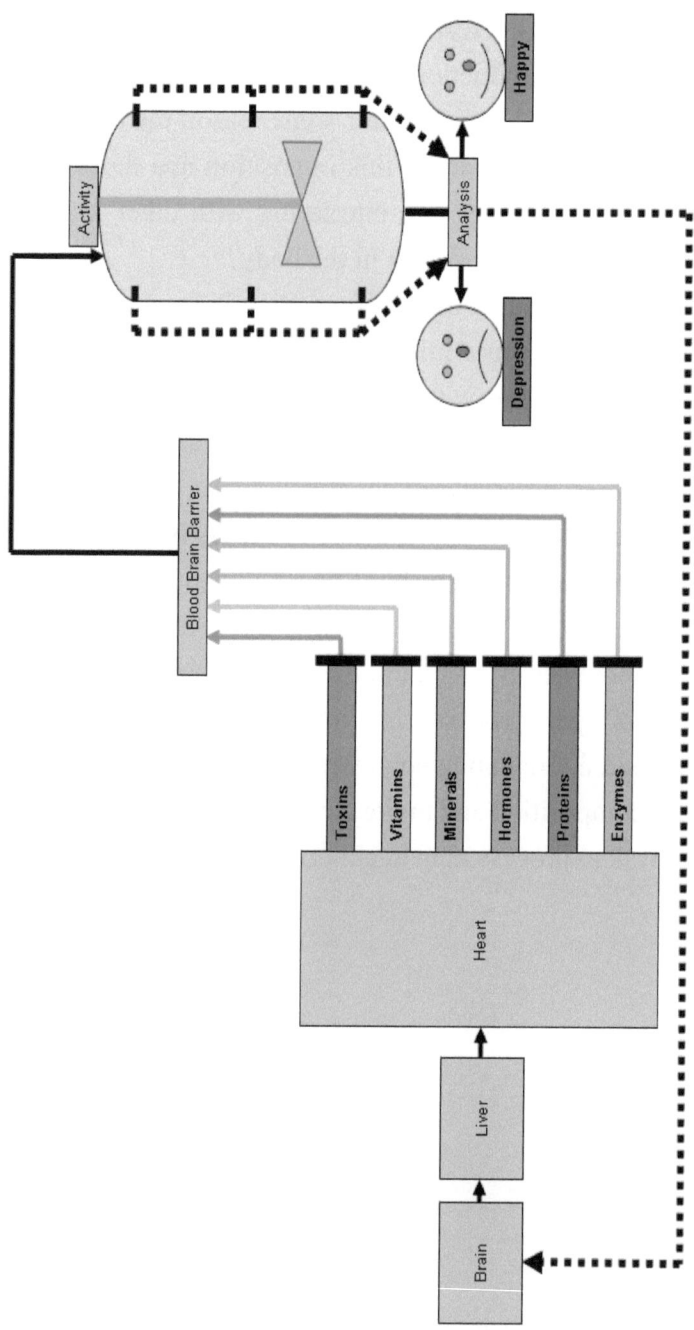

At the point I began to understand my realities I knew my life would change

What I'm talking about is the successful formula for the presentation of deep depression and possibly suicidal depression. Now that's not rocket science is it? Neither is it to preposterous to be true. Well I'm afraid if you talk to anyone from the medical industry about this proposition they will immediately poo poo it and why? Well:

(a) They haven't got a clue.

And

(b) How dare you raise the spectre that you know what's going on in you; they're the expert, not you.

I have a magnificent body that supports me in all my endeavours

Okay so I covered the body's inability to recover and repair itself as a matter of course. Now I want to touch upon another area that really pisses me off. It's the area of disproportionate empathetic illness connection that we, who are chronically ill, frequently encounter. It's those silly people who try to apply and impose the recovery logic of their past shallow medical impositions upon us. Now reading this book it might be difficult to accept that I once was a very gentle man, a highly spiritual man because I'm the first to agree that there is a lot of liver anger or cathartic cleansing coming through in the theme of this book. Nevertheless I was funnily enough a *very* spiritual man once upon a time and because of that I met and knew lots of people on their own unique spiritual paths. Some used it as a crutch, others used it as a point of social contact, some used it to explain away their idiosyncratic flaws, some used it as a foundation for growth and some were quite simply charlatans and frauds.

The reason I'm covering the so called enlightened dimension is because to some who are chronically ill, perhaps as their condition declines, their only points of contact will be with those of so-called an enlightened inclination.

You see, we all need someone to talk to and to feel that there is a reason and a season for everything, that's just the way it is. Even the biggest unbelievers amongst us will cry out to their God at the point another man holds a gun to their head. But there is a real danger lurking in the midst of the spiritually enlightened brigade. There is a culture of acceptance, of assigning conditions to some form of spiritual lesson, of not fighting the condition but letting it beat you. If I had £10's for every time some 'so called enlighten dude' said to me 'give it up to the universe Baz you're choosing to suffer and struggle' I would be driving a brand new Porsche not relying upon public transport.

At the point I began to understand my realities I knew my life would change

The give it up to the universe thing is absolute bloody rubbish and what's worse is that its invariably offered to you from a platform of projected great understanding when in reality there is little understanding at all.

Let me tell you where I am on this sort of shit, I would frequently say to my best friend John, there must be a reason for this pal and yet his pragmatic West Cumbrian reply was always this, 'perhaps not Baz, perhaps shit just happens and you're just getting more than your fair share of the shit marra'. Now John was not a spiritual sort of guy he was just a very decent and honourable guy of that there was never any doubt. His reply was as pragmatic as he'd been blessed in living his life. But when I postulated my view to members of the spiritual brigade their retort was frequently, 'let go of your ego Baz, your choosing to suffer, just give it up to the universe etc, etc, etc'. Now the reason that still rankles me even to this day is that I knew those people more than they thought I did and I could see their hypocrisies deep within. Soft music, candles, joss sticks, beans and lentils but give them the slightest problem and their whole world came tumbling in around the shallow façade they'd built for themselves. Yet there they were listening but not hearing my despair, quoting verbatim extracts from anyone of a number of inspirational ways of being books that they'd just read, telling me I must do something and then by subtle innuendo placing the blame for my condition back onto me. It's simply preposterous to think that if we do nothing we will have:

(a) Completed one of our karmic challenges.

And

(c) That perhaps our condition will sort itself out if it's truly meant to be.

I have a magnificent body that supports me in all my endeavours

What if we solve the problem ourselves surely we've solved the karmic challenge and won't need to do it again. Also in solving the problem we've given our body the sort of help and support that it needed or needs. Look, if I have chronic toothache:

- Do I have chronic toothache?

Or

- Is that a karmic lesson?

If I give my chronic toothache up to the universe, does the universe hear me and does it take my pain away? Well the answers are:

- Of course I have a toothache be that of a karmic or physical nature who really cares?

But

- Sitting and waiting for something to happen from a divine perspective is not going to take my pain away.

My tooth needs dental intervention, be that an extraction or repair and when I'm feeling much better I can consider the karmic scheme of things whilst taking better care of my teeth. Now look the point I've caustically emphasized here is, if anyone ever says to you give your condition up to the universe or you're choosing to suffer from depression, look them straight in the eyes and tell them to 'fuck right off'.

At the point I began to understand my realities I knew my life would change

The road to depression expression diagnosis and recovery can be tortuous and slow, but at the point we begin to accept the bigger scheme of things, that's the very same point we begin to regroup our perceptions and thoughts. We begin to understand the complexity of depression, the many systems and issues that we need to address simply to enable ourselves to be completely depression free. I couldn't possibly cover all the complex components of depression in this book including, toxins, disease, hormones, inflammation and histamines etc, but I hope my insights and perceptions have at least simulated your own thoughts.

I have a magnificent body that supports me in all my endeavours

Before I sign this chapter off let me leave you with one final thought in terms of my differing views on the expression of depression. You see; when I was a young guy growing up in the small town of Whitehaven, there was an expression that was used in a matter of fact sort of way and that was; every time we were greeted with a bright full moon. People would look to the sky and jokingly say; 'Bloody hell, the 'A ward' and 'police station' will be full tonight marra' and what's more they were frequently right. The same families, every time there was a bright full moon, would be involved in some sort of ruckus, the same guys would be done for drunk and disorderly matters and the same guys would be lifted and carted off to the local psychiatric 'A ward'. Because time after time the same people would experience subtle changes in their personality every time we had a full moon.

Big joke eh! People were referred to as wolf men and satirized all their lives. When in reality it was no joke and the reason why it was no joke is because those changes in their personalities were completely outside of their rational control. All of them I suggest had some form of DNA, placenta transferred, ingested or sexually transmitted parasitical, viral or fungal infestation which meant every twenty eight days they experienced an event known simply as hatching. You see there are no coincidences in terms of emotive reactions and depressive expression during full moons etc.

Those actions are the result of increased toxin loads brought about by parasitical hatchings which are always in tune with our moon's cycle. I know from personal experience only too well how those hatching cycles can affect us, because that's the approximate cycle of Lymes Disease etc. So you see, there are so many things that can exert a depressive expression upon us, which means that the key to our well being must always be to simply note and record our body's expression of disease.

At the point I began to understand my realities I knew my life would change

For over time we're then able to profile our disease, hence removing all the delusions and illusions that we've allowed ourselves to buy into, by simply using my process logic map below as an aide-memoir.

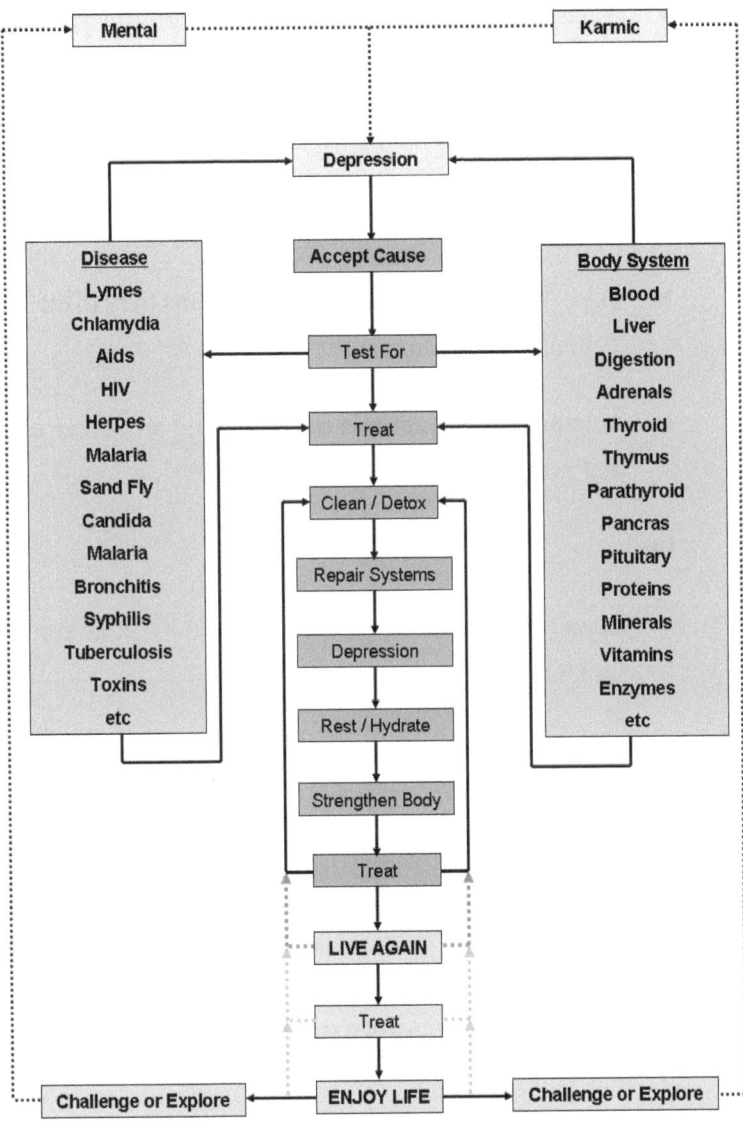

Does a man move into depression expression because of the state of his mind or is he pushed into depression expression because of the state of his body? – YOUR CHOICE !

I have a magnificent body that supports me in all my endeavours

With reference to this simple process logic map it's important that you take control of all your diseased state expressions and if one of those expressions is that of depression, then your choices are:

- Accept the spiritual suggestions of giving your problem up to the universe.

- Accept the diagnosis offered by your medics.

- Determine how you're going to follow their advice.

- Take the medications and suggestions they offer and stick to that treatment regime.

- Accept all eventualities from any and all course of actions that you take.

Or

- Reject the words of wisdom offered by your spiritual associates.

- Reject the diagnosis offered by your medics.

- Explore the potential of multiple impositions.

- Commit to taking complete ownership of your pursuit of well being.

- Accept all eventualities from any and all course of actions that you take.

At the point I began to understand my realities I knew my life would change

EXPLORING OBSESSIVE COMPULSIVE DISORDER PRAGMATICALLY

Exploration Ten

I have a magnificent body that supports me in all my endeavours

At the point I began to understand my realities I knew my life would change

Throughout my life I've struggled with the words; Passionate, Obsession and Addicted, because whilst all can have positive connotations equally they all can have negative connotations when either misunderstood or counterproductive to what society dictates is an acceptable standard. So let's have a look at those words and then explore how they are bastardized by society.

- Passionate; 'capable of revealing or characterized by intense emotion'.

- Obsession; 'state of persistent idea or impulse'.

- Addicted; 'person devoted to something'.

I have a magnificent body that supports me in all my endeavours

From a very young age I realised that I had the potential to be passionate, obsessive and even addictive. Yet in the most part the prejudices that surrounded me qualified those traits as negative and self destructive traits and not at all helpful, controlled or informed states. A formative, yet negative neuro-linguistic programming culture which meant that at the point I moved into a chronic diseased state and became chronically obsessive I bought into albeit only on one level, all the negative clap trap I'd been spun about obsession etc.

Now there can be nothing worse than living in a body when your mind is in a chronic obsessive state because that mind set takes you to places where you really shouldn't have to go at all. It's a place where destructive and counterproductive thoughts all but drive you insane. Those thoughts can range from self harm, to; chronic fear, physical detachment, delusion, thoughts of harming others and a raft of thoughts which are both irrational and counterproductive to acceptable standards in terms of quality of life. Chronic obsession can consume and destroy any and all sense of reality and whilst in a chronic obsessive state we are at the mercy of all our obsessive thoughts which in the most part are completely without validity or rationale.

Now the reason I jumped straight to the obsessive state is because I believe that we all need to soften our views on what constitutes Passionate, Obsessive and Addicted mind sets, because I believe all three states are one in the same. To change our perceptions however, we first must view all three with equal polarity. In doing so we can begin to understand the part they all play in the mortal process of stimulation, progression, stagnation and/or degeneration and any point in our lives.

At the point I began to understand my realities I knew my life would change

Some of our greatest and worst role models have their roots based firmly in a personal predisposition towards intense emotions. They believe and believed with passion and are or were not afraid to air their views. It is that predisposition that seems to set them apart from their kin. Interestingly passionate individuals have the potential to both stimulate and antagonize populist beliefs with equal equity. Yet it is the shift in perceptions generated by passionate individuals that either causes buy-in to change or stimulates rejection which by default brings about paradoxical change.

But what you may ask has passion to do with obsession or addiction? Well I would argue that passion without obsessive or addictive traits doesn't really exist. In fact I would go as far as to say that all three dispositions are nothing more than derivations of a Driven Life Force (DLF). But DLF should not be confused with Divine Life Forces because the former is physical presence where as the later is spiritual higher presence.

I believe that it is the driven life force within us all that we need to understand because at the point we understand the generators and markers of DLF then perhaps we can begin to understand the subtle delineation between positive and negative manifestation of DLF. Or should I say the positive and negative presentations of Passionate, Obsessive and Addicted mind states.

You see; we are all nothing more than a complex mix of water, carbon and chemicals and yet it is that soup and its formulation that makes us the people we think we are. Some of us may feel inferior, troubled or even superior at any time or point in our life. But the bottom line at the end of the day is that our perception of who we are, is nothing more than a projection derived from the soup we either inherit or we've somehow managed to manipulate or corrupt during our passage through

I have a magnificent body that supports me in all my endeavours

life. I argue that it is the constitution or subtle changes to the generators and markers of DLF that enables us to be both accepted and acceptable to society as a whole or alienate ourselves wholesale. DLF by default generates presence, it orchestrates great change, it challenges perceptions whilst retaining at its very core the self preservation which is that most unique facet that underwrites us all and the one thing that eventually generates the most conflict.

There is no issue for me in terms of the major components of DLF they are of course Passionate, Obsessive and Addicted mind sets. Therefore I believe that whoever has the constituent generators and marker of visible DLF will automatically demonstrate either in illness or good health; Passionate, Obsessive and Addictive mind sets.

Now whilst I accept the potential for everyone to have some degree of DLF presentation, I'm nevertheless of the opinion that active DLF is seen only in the minority and not the majority. I also believe its needs to be that way otherwise cohabiting on a global scale in a soup rich with DLF mind sets would be very challenging to say the very least.

For it is DLF mind sets that challenge and change the world we live in and be under no illusion about that, simply because DFL's view the components of life in more detail than their peers. Therein they push themselves harder than their peers; they are less prepared to go with the flow than their peers. Alarmingly at times however they present greater fluidity in the linear magnitude of their positive and negative DLF mind state and statements of intent.

At the point I began to understand my realities I knew my life would change

DLF's are energized individuals so that when we explore DLF mind sets its clear that;

- A lazy man can never be a DLF because his very acceptance and preposition to being lazy indicates that passion and a passionate mind set are missing from him. It's simply impossible to be passionate about being lazy no matter what anyone says because to be passionate requires tremendous energy in mind and body. Therefore if a man has that and not simply using words then it's impossible for him to be lazy.

- Equally obsession requires tremendous energy; therefore those of a more sedate mind set are probably devoid of obsessive generators and marker because it's impossible to be sedentary amidst the stimulation of obsession.

- Addiction on the other hand has both a passive and active component to it; nevertheless I argue that to fall into an addictive mind set there must first be either an active enquiring or a generally unsettled mind, which is the primary drive I would respectfully suggest of a DLF in all its presentations.

DLF mind sets are extremely active and energized individuals; and I argue that it is that energetic expression of intent that manifests in both positive and negative expression in a DLF. Let me give you two diametrically opposite examples of DLF;

I have a magnificent body that supports me in all my endeavours

- Margaret Thatcher and Adolph Hitler clearly had intense DLF, they both had great presence, both had great passion, both had great obsessions, both demonstrated addictive personalities towards power, both had the ability to engage the populous and yet both had the potential of demonstrating gross cruelty which was seemingly justifiable in their minds whilst amassing great personal wealth at others expense. This I would suggest is negative DLF.

- Alfred Einstein and Isambard Kingdom Brunel clearly had intense DLF, they both had great presence, both had great passion, both had great obsessions, both demonstrated addictive personalities, both had the ability to engage the populous and both had the potential to endure great personal sacrifice in pursuit of their ideals. This I would suggest is positive DLF.

The problem some may argue is that both the negative and positive DLF's that I've just presented are nothing more than subjective derivatives of my own personal prejudices. Well that is the very point I'm attempting to make.

You see in the vast majority of instances where society expresses a view on Passionate, Obsessive and/or Addicted mind states, those subsequent assessments are always from points of personal prejudices and not from holistic clinical assessment.

It's very obvious to me that in differing times and differing situations both Margaret Thatcher and Adolph Hitler would have been devoid of any real power and actually considered lunatics and despicable mortals because of their propensity towards negative DLF. But they weren't at the most important time in their own personal history and that's what's really most important. Because perceptions are transient, subjective and frequently in tune with similar opportunist mind sets.

You see negative DFL's frequently have the ability to self propel their views by connecting with and manipulating the age old problem of collective acceptance of the unacceptable for fear of alienation or reprisal and/or buy-in to jingoistic zealous dogma from self interested DLF's. It is only at the point that they lose that connective populist alignment that the dynamic and perception of who they are, what they say and what they stand for is subject to; differing cognitive analysis.

Now I've sort of laboured that point because it is an important point in that I argue that what constitutes acceptable mind traits today may not always be deemed acceptable tomorrow and visa versa. In that our perceptions of who we are and the traits that we align ourselves to; do not have any other significance save for presenting themselves through the DLF that is unique to our body state at any given moment in time.

I have a magnificent body that supports me in all my endeavours

We may well have a clearly defined sense of our personality or mind state traits by the time we're in our mid teens etc. But in reality none of us truly know what the generators and markers of our DLF actually are. Because of that its therefore possible; to buy-in to formative neuro-linguistic programming perceptions of our DLF which can be counterproductive when for whatever reason our DLF moves further into either a positive or negative presentation of our understanding of what we believe is our base presenting DLF state. The result of that is we either big ourselves up or write ourselves off or we try to hide from what we're experiencing or thinking and eventually buy-in to perceptions of who and what we are in the complete absence of clinical diagnosis. I know that from personal experience that at the point chronic long term illness brings us to our knees we don't really know who we are anymore and are vulnerable to believe anything postulated as being in our best interests.

Be under no illusion that at the point our DLF moves into a perceived negative state, society in general begins to perceive our DLF to be an expression of some form of psychiatric condition. Now whilst that may be true in some instances I would argue that negative DLF is nothing more than an expression of imbalance in the soup that underpins normalized DFL states. Therefore I argue that we cannot correct that DLF expression with self beasting, simplistic or puerile drug treatment approaches. The only way to correct that is to analyse and determine the underlying causes of the deviations to our DLF.

You see, I frequently read about fallen stars and people who have been written off as having addictive and obsessive personalities and at one point in my life I bought into that perception myself. But I don't believe in that anymore because I believe that all mind states and cravings etc, are nothing more than impositions or deficiencies being imposed either directly or indirectly upon the soup that underpins our DLF.

At the point I began to understand my realities I knew my life would change

We cannot ingest or be exposed to poisons or diseased states without them having a direct impact upon our DLF. Therefore when our DLF moves in a significant direction its imperative that we understand why that is, but we can only do that if we accept that DLF normalization can only be achieved through whole body view determination.

I simply don't accept now that negative DLF's in whatever presentation they take form e.g. obsessive compulsive disorder, sexual deviancy, drugs, obesity, violent conduct or alcohol etc, are based purely upon inherited mind states or predispositions. I believe the root of all those conditions lay in the soup that underpins normalized DLF's. If that soup is genetically corrupted in the first instance and/or we are exposed to factors that contribute to the disruption to concentrations of generators and markers to normalized DLF's then extremes of DLF expression is obviously going to be the ultimate outcome.

I therefore believe that it's time to stop all self beasting, all the poor me bullshit that we frequently allow ourselves to believe e.g. 'O my this was this and my that was that and that's why I am like I am etc'. But I say that only because I once allowed myself to believe all that crap and the fact of the matter is that in that mind set we only hold ourselves back.

There are many many things that move our DLF's from one extreme to another not least of which is life itself. But if we are ever to be in a positive DLF state it's important to note that positive DLF's cannot be found in medication or substance ingestion unless we've identified in the first instance the actual root cause.

You see; the bodily soups that underpin our very existence are responsible for all our perceptions and sense of reality. For it's that given and that given alone which drives all our focus and clarity of mind.

I have a magnificent body that supports me in all my endeavours

That being said, we cannot possibly move from a functioning individual into someone racked by chronic DFL unless some form of corruption has played a part in the constitution of our DFL soup. When we stop viewing Passionate, Obsessive and Addicted mind sets in prejudiced, intransigent, single polarity values of positive and negative then we begin to understand who we are.

You see; a positive is of no use without a negative for we need both to ensure balance. Maintaining a balanced DLF however is a challenge because our DLF is always in a state of flux as the subtle changes to the constituents of our DLF soup ebb and flow. A balanced DLF is therefore by no means prescriptively set at some predefined intransigent position; it is as fluid as the universe we inhabit. The key however to individual and collective understanding of DLF is to accept the need to manage and not marginalize the concept and reality of the Driven Life Force that we all have the potential to hold.

We have a personal obligation if we wish to move to a healthy DLF to drive the determination of all DLF soup corrupting factors and not simply accept that there is nothing that we or anyone else can do to change an unhealthy DLF to a healthy DLF. The choice as ever remains firmly with us because we are the custodians of our DLF's. I accepted long ago that I'm a DLF, that's why I fought with all my might for better health, that's why I fight every single day of my life against ignorance of mind, body and soul. I have a DLF inside me which ensures that at all times I'm in touch and can access all my full potential.

At the point I began to understand my realities I knew my life would change

Where are you now in terms of your DLF positioning? Well if you need help in determining that have a look through my simple DLF management tool below, who knows it could be the making of you.

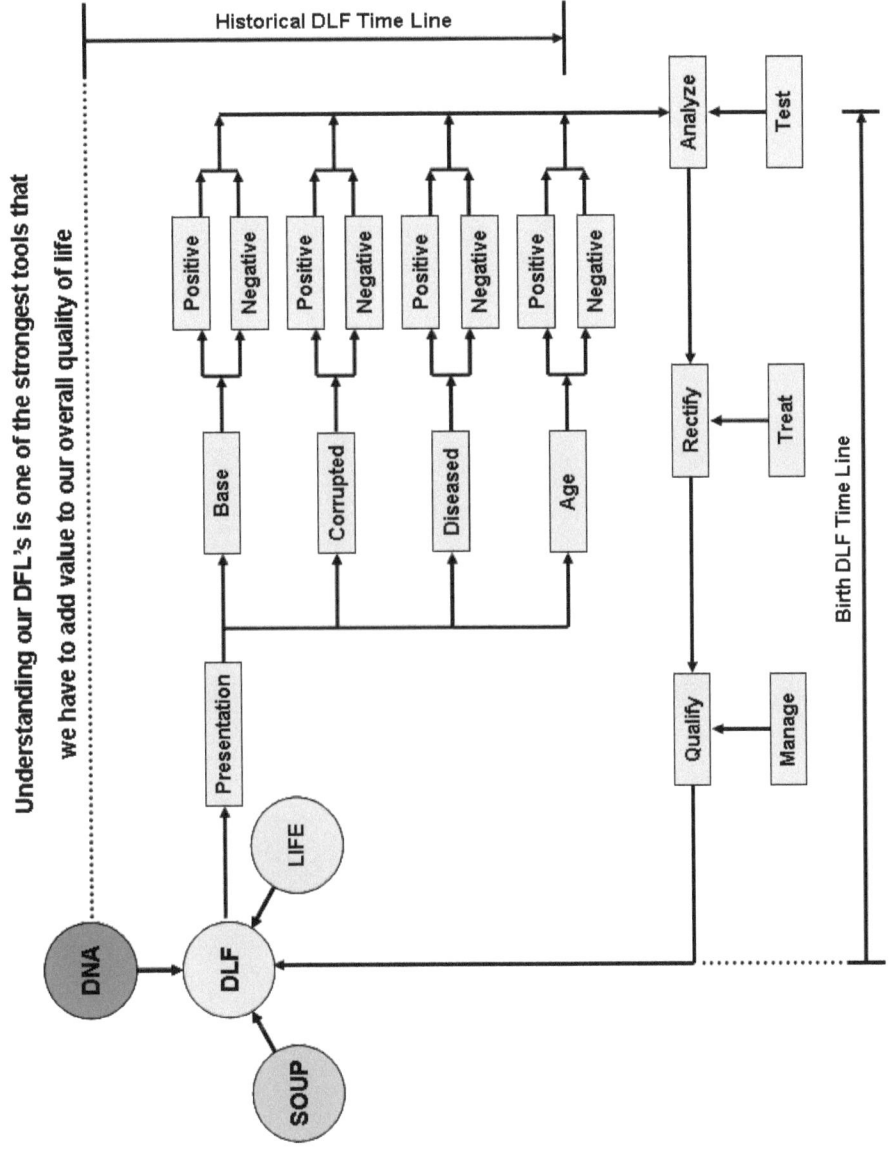

I have a magnificent body that supports me in all my endeavours

At the point I began to understand my realities I knew my life would change

EXPLORING ANALYTICAL TESTING PRAGMATICALLY

Exploration Eleven

I have a magnificent body that supports me in all my endeavours

At the point I began to understand my realities I knew my life would change

It's fair to say that some of us really go through the mill several times before our illness is finally diagnosed, yet at the point we're diagnosed we then hopefully via an effective treatment regime, can begin to make a substantive recovery from our presenting conditions. Sadly however, some of us actually never recover and that's primarily due to two reasons:

- Our condition is terminal.

- Or analytical sciences and clinical investigations are simply unable to detect a problem.

Ironically, during my baron chronic illness resolution days, whilst I was failed wholesale by UK analytical sciences and clinical investigations, I was diagnosed as terminally ill in the USA. How strange is that?

Well not that strange really when you scratch the surface of analytical sciences and clinical investigations in the UK. You see, the vast majority of tests, machines, and imaging devices that we have in the UK are not state of the art as the industry or our government would like us to believe. They're actually state of the ark. It's not until you actually analyse the state of that medical service sector that you find out just how bad things really are.

I have a magnificent body that supports me in all my endeavours

A situation compounded further by the front end medical cretins who request investigations and then either play a part or choose to abstain from interpolating any subsequent results objectively leaving us as the sufferer bemused.

I really don't think there can be anything worse than having a major health impediment and yet because of out dated and fundamentally flawed analytical sciences and clinical investigations no one can find anything wrong with you. At that point despite your intense suffering you're simply written off as a neurotic and the most alarming thing is that there is no difference either between the NHS and the private sector.

Time after time I've paid for very expensive consultations and tests and time after time some pompous, greedy, ignorant 'medical rogue' has said to me, 'actually there's nothing wrong with you your tests are normal Mr. Hardy' Followed by, 'have you considered psychiatric help?'

Equally in the NHS I've been abused in far too many situations by 'medical rogues' saying, 'Mr. Hardy there's absolutely nothing wrong with you it's all in your head' and their other favourite line, 'Mr. Hardy we can't keep on testing you why can't you just accept that you have a mental health issue?'

It is primarily because of all the rubbish and abuse I've had to endure that I advocate that we must take control of this situation. How dare some talentless, badly trained yet public sector worker say that the NHS can't keep testing me or anyone of us? I've / we've funded their bloody training, I / we've funded their bloody life styles and some of us have battled to preserve their bloody rotten industry from the ravages of Thatcherism. Boy do those 'charlatans' really make me angry.

At the point I began to understand my realities I knew my life would change

You see, I really don't give a hoot if the NHS has to perform a thousand bloody tests upon me to find out what's wrong with me, that's what it's there for and therefore that's what it needs to do. Or it could certainly begin in the name of greater efficiencies, to look at the amount of money it's wasting on fundamentally flawed analytical sciences and clinical investigations and start bring its house in order.

Because if some clerical or 'clinical rogue' is assigning limits to the level of care that I can have from the NHS, then I for one now say let's have voluntary contributions to the NHS. Why should I a potential high earner pay ridiculous amounts of money to underwrite an industry that doesn't want to underwrite me when I need it? Yet it throws billions away on consultant's salaries and treats any chancer who decides to pop over to the UK for treatment.

Now hey I would never in a million years have thought that this working class lad from Woodhouse would ever have held such views towards the NHS. But having been exposed head on to all its woeful underperformance, ignorance and incompetence for years, I'm happy to voice my harsh views now. My belief now is that we need to bring this entire rotten industry crashing to its knees. So that as a nation we're able to build a clinical care service sector that is thorough, competitive; inspirational and world class and let's ditch the clap trap and rubbish of the past.

I have a magnificent body that supports me in all my endeavours

The problem with that vision is that the people who have suffered most from its shoddy service are unfortunately the ones with the lowest vitality, presence or voice. So before any of its victims can commit to campaigning for change they need to get well for only then can they hope to bring about change. But be under no illusion that dynamic changes quickly at the point our health returns. Unfortunately the road to recovery can be lonely, long and unrewarding at times and so until we reach our desired destination, its best for all chronically ill patients to focus solely upon regaining their health and leave the clinical reform campaign to better times.

Prior to our return to health however, let me give you a flavour of what happens in the normal psyche when we're experiencing a health condition and require analytical sciences and/or clinical investigations. We immediately make either a big or small deal of the fact that our condition is going to be subject to further scrutiny. Some of us may be worried that something dreadful may be found, whilst others may simply be happy if something could be found to enable us to be treated, recover and move on. I've always come from the school of thought, 'I hope they can find something so that I could move on'. I've never subscribed to worrying about there being something dreadfully wrong with me, because I only ever wanted solutions. I knew for years that I had something seriously wrong with me; I just didn't know what it was. If we don't know what's wrong with us then we can't ever hope to recover and in poor health, recovery must be our sole interest if we wish to regain some form of quality of life. Therefore we must commit to testing and analytical investigations and when the results come through, we must do our level best to acknowledge them and deal with them as appropriately as we're able to or at the very least, see fit.

At the point I began to understand my realities I knew my life would change

So let's play the cycle through now, our test results come back and they're always in the standard form of:

- (a) Your tests are normal.
- (b) Hmmn, there is a slight problem but that might just be congenital.
- (c) You have bla bla bla bla.
- (d) You need to make an appointment to discuss your results.

Now to understand the ramifications of that feedback we need to look at the two generic psyches I discussed earlier i.e. big or small deal propensity. So let's look at the big deal psyche first:

(a) Results normal = maybe happy deep down and prepared to take whatever the medical representative says in terms of treatments etc., but may ham it up a bit when speaking to colleagues, family and friends.

(b) Result might be a congenital issue = may be worried deep down yet prepared to take whatever the medical representative says in terms of treatments etc. Might however blow the condition completely out of proportion and will certainly ham it up a bit when speaking to colleagues, family and friends.

(c) Result you have bla bla = may be extremely worried and also might blow the condition completely out of proportion until reassured by the medic, but will certainly ham it up a lot when speaking to colleagues, family and friends.

I have a magnificent body that supports me in all my endeavours

(d) Result you need a follow up appointment = extremely worried and will blow the condition completely out of proportion, because that brings the drama they crave into their life. As long as it's a safe and controllable drama that's fine, should it however not be a safe drama then they will start off being publicly very brave and then simply implode putting tremendous pressure on anyone in close proximity.

At the point I began to understand my realities I knew my life would change

So let's look at the small deal psyche now:

(a) Results normal = maybe confused deep down but prepared to take to some extent whatever the medical representative says.

(b) Result might be a congenital issue = may be worried but certainly interested in the result more from a clinical perspective than a sensationalist perspective.

(c) Result you have bla bla = may be worried but happy that there is something to discuss, but will need answers.

(d) Result you need a follow up appointment = worried until they understand what's wrong with them, but once they know they just get their heads down with it and are normally stronger than the people around them, who sometimes fall to pieces.

I have a magnificent body that supports me in all my endeavours

Now look it doesn't really matter what personality type you fall into. The key to returning to optimum health is ensuring that you're either prepared to be driven or you're prepared to drive the situation. Either way your focus must be upon achieving optimum health, because if you're not experiencing optimum health then you need to understand why; assuming that is that optimum health is your real goal. I've postulated that we must all examine if optimum health is our real goal, and I raise that challenging point because whilst some people will say optimum health is their goal. You only have to talk or listen to them to understand that they are indeed lost or closed to the potential of optimum health. That is because some people really do like being ill, because in being ill they:

- Have the crutch they need.

- Don't need to compete.

- Can offload all their personal issues at the door of their illness or disease.

At the point I began to understand my realities I knew my life would change

Now there is absolutely no crime in that, save to say, if a man does not wish to help himself, then perhaps help is not what he needs. You see there are no secrets to optimum health save for a desire to have optimum health, yet within that expectation and desire there are many levels of acceptance and abstinence. Only we as individuals have the sole right to make the value judgments that best meet our desires and needs.

My personal expectations have always been to secure a quality of life that is free from physical impediments and diseased states. Because of that I've mapped a holistic yet pragmatic approach to this process on the next page, now whilst it may initially look complex when you first see it. Just take time to follow some of the evolution and iteration loops from your own perspective and you'll find that it caters precisely for whichever mind set you are.

I have a magnificent body that supports me in all my endeavours

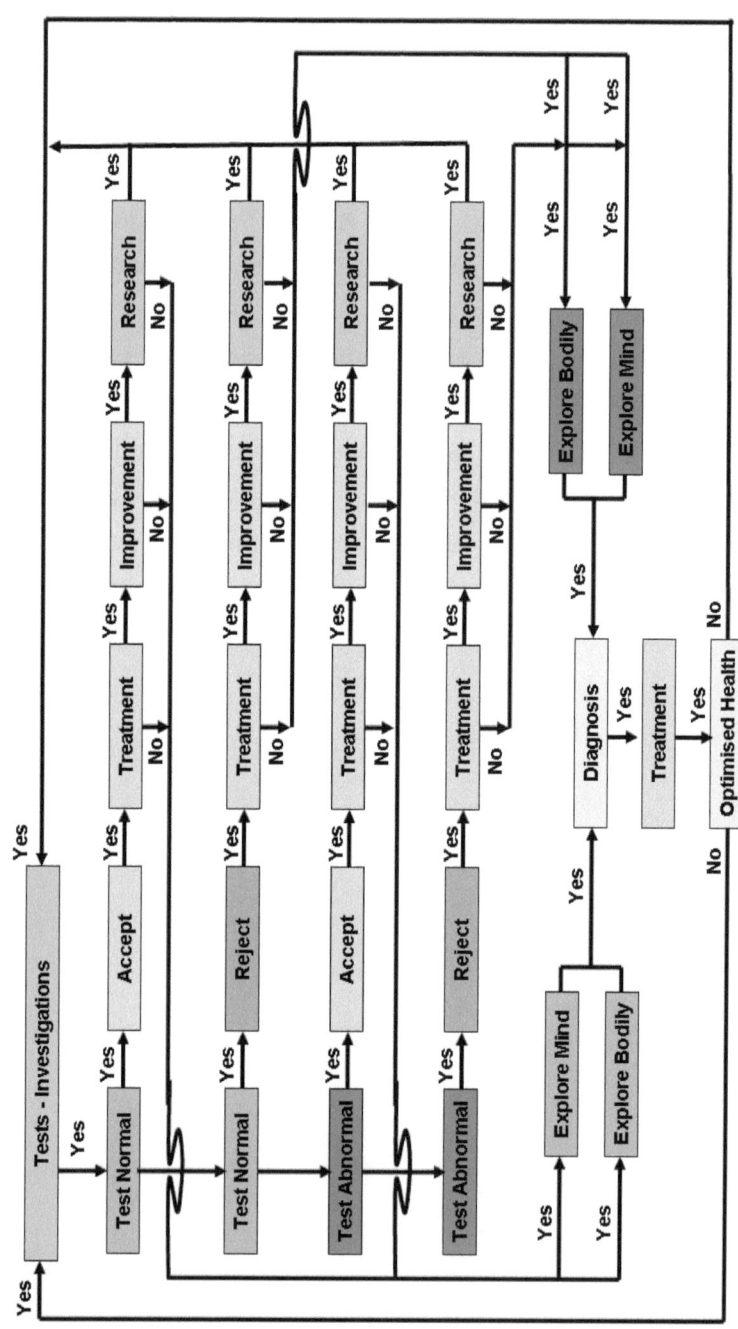

At the point I began to understand my realities I knew my life would change

During my pre-diagnostic state my only abstinences were to reject wholesale any and all forms of clap trap or ignorantly manufactured dogma articulated to distract me from my goal. I advocate only this that in the pursuit of optimum health we all must accept that we alone are the responsible party for driving the process of recovery through diagnosis. For without our input, there is no other form of input worthy of comment and therefore no reasonable probability of making any form of sustainable recovery.

Yet whilst that is, or can be, a very difficult path for some of us to walk alone, in reality it's the only path that delivers access to clarity, understanding, effective treatment and recovery. It is by default however; a process of two stages, the first stage is the stage where we are in essence ignorant and unable to make progress because we rely completely upon false testing, consultations and investigations which have little if any merit. I've mapped that process for you on the next page, because once we understand all the loops in the process, it is no longer a mystery and can indeed become that defining point from which we all move forward.

I have a magnificent body that supports me in all my endeavours

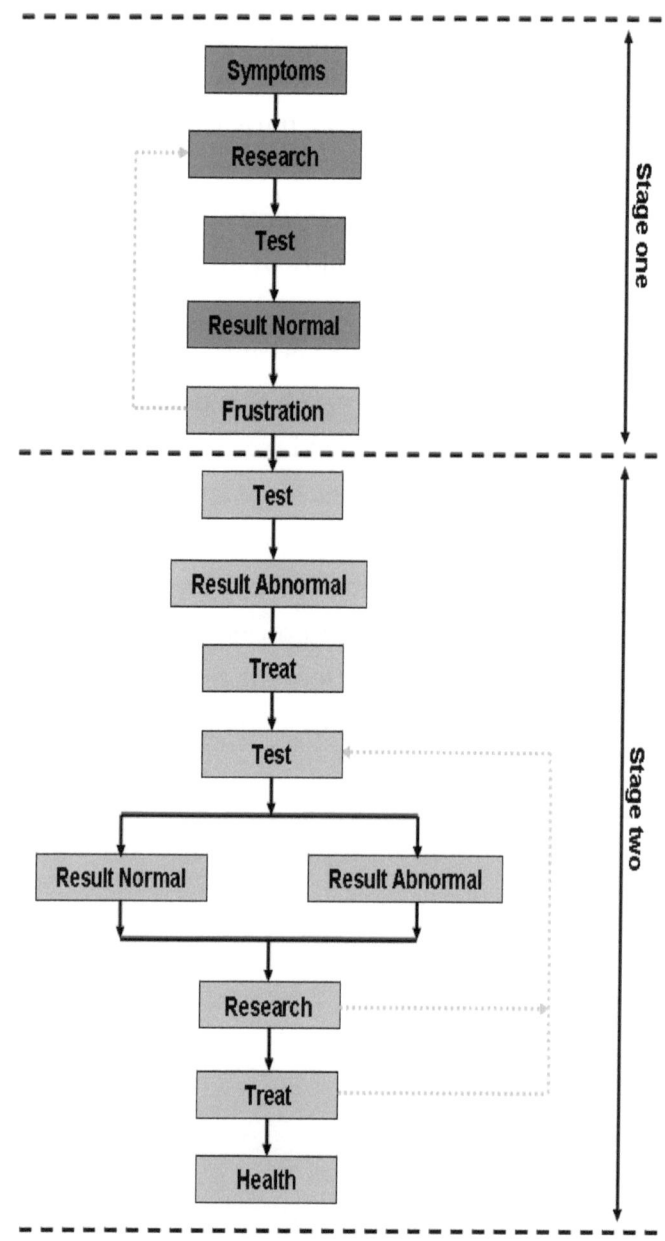

Ignore the doubters who say you can't keep on testing you can and you must

At the point I began to understand my realities I knew my life would change

The second stage is where we take ownership of the intellect responsibility for substantiating our underlying condition or conditions. It is the point that we start unravelling our health mysteries, that remarkable point where we see the medical industry and those who support it for what and who they really are.

Both stages are incredibly difficult because they are both encountered when we have lower than normal vitality. Stage one will invariably consist of a 90% - 10% NHS and private involvement whereas 'stage two' will be the complete opposite i.e. 10% - 90% NHS and private involvement.

Therefore there are significant cost implications required of those attempting to return to a position of optimum health. Some of that money will be wasted and some of it will be money well spent. There is no right or wrong course of action to take, all we can ever be is true to ourselves and whilst we can't beat the obscene and perverse nature of the medical industry. We can get better through our own efforts and eventually realise our dreams if only we're prepared to drive the testing and analysis until a reflective diagnosis has been achieved. In my particular situation stage one of my investigation process consisted of nothing more than the following fundamentally flawed investigations below:

- 3 Liver enzyme tests.
- 3 Thyroid tests.
- 1 MRI.
- 1 CT.
- 1 X-ray investigation.

I have a magnificent body that supports me in all my endeavours

The conclusions drawn from them were that I was fine and had nothing wrong with me except for mental health issues, time and time again. Whereas my stage two self funded investigations included:

- 5 MRI's.

- 2 MRA's.

- 4 CAT scans.

- 2 CT's.

- 60+ blood tests and bodily function analysis, tests and examinations.

- 9 Caloric Tests.

- 3 Hearing Tests.

- 9 ENG Tests.

- Two Neurosurgical procedures.

- 180+ clinical consultations all around the world plus travel and accommodation.

- Plus thousands of hours research on the internet long before cheap broad band, etc.

- In summation personal traceable costs in excess of 300K.

At the point I began to understand my realities I knew my life would change

The result of my tenacity in the face of unbelievable odds was that I was eventually diagnosed with:

- Chronic late stage Lymes Disease.

- Chronic mitochondria failure.

- Chronic liver disease.

- Chronic adrenal insufficiency.

- And an extremely rare genetic yet organic anomaly resulting in a Posterior Inferior Cerebella Artery insulting my vestibular bundle and brain stem left side. *Note this condition still imposes great suffering upon me every minute of every day and that's why just putting my thoughts onto paper is such an almighty affair.*

Now look, the point I'm making is that there are far too many issues surrounding our poor medical investigation model and too many issues surrounding outdated machines and devices being postulated as state of the art diagnostic tools. How many of us actually know until we are faced with horrendous medical conditions just how bad the equipment and techniques used to analyse our bodies truly are through-out the nhs because if we did I'm sure our own dogs of war would be unleashed.

I have a magnificent body that supports me in all my endeavours

How many of us have been for an MRI scan and been told that everything is normal, when in reality the MRI scanner being used is:

- Badly designed and maintained?

- Outdated and malfunctioning?

- An expensive piece of scrap metal?

- Operated by people who don't give a shit.

Now we all know the difference between top and low end motoring in terms of performance etc, but very few of us know that the same is the case in the medical industry. You see, in the push to kid us all into thinking our health is safe in their hands, NHS trusts all around the country installed sub standard equipment which in the majority of instances are nothing more than token gestures in terms of world class clinical investigation tools. The differences are so wide in terms of performing basic functions that it's like giving one man a set of binoculars and another an electron microscope to analyse the same bacteria, now that would be simply ridiculous wouldn't it?

Well the truth is, the state of our nation's clinical diagnostic tools is not simply ridiculous, it's actually a disgrace and we the front end users or mugs are the ones paying the highest price. We're sent for diagnostic investigations, the results come back normal and the result of that is, no further line of investigation undertaken despite the fact that your condition may continue to decline.

At the point I began to understand my realities I knew my life would change

Simply because a shit piece of equipment operated by people who don't give a shit has indicating that you have no problem or in point of fact is unable to detect the problem you have. Now I sincerely hope that my observations through suffering and personal wasted expense has set off some alarm bells deep within you because those alarm bells need to resonate with us all as a society each and every day because we need this resolved not next year or next month I would respectfully suggest but tomorrow and it must happen before lunch time at the very latest.

Because I advocate that when and where there is evidence to suggest that the instruments, techniques, systems and protocols used to support clinical investigations are incapable of investigating with the degree of enquiry that we need, then we need to:

- Challenge the results.

- Find suitable systems etc, which can perform to the level and standard of integrity that we require.

You see, I'm no solo foot soldier here, millions of us are being written off every year by fundamentally flawed medical investigations, consultations and tests. So if you truly desire optimum health, you're going to have to fight for it with all your intellect, strength and might. You're going to have to:

- Ignore the personal and clinical prejudices that you encounter.

- You're going to have to spend money that you may not have.

- You're going to have to prove your condition yourself.

I have a magnificent body that supports me in all my endeavours

Because if you think for one moment that the state, the NHS or our private medical health circus will resolve anything more than a superficial health impediment then your sadly mistaken because they won't. Only you can drive this stage two part of your pursuit of disease expression reflective diagnosis, because in reality there really only is you who truly gives a damn. So to help keep you upbeat and focused during that process I've mapped a very simple process approach plan for you below.

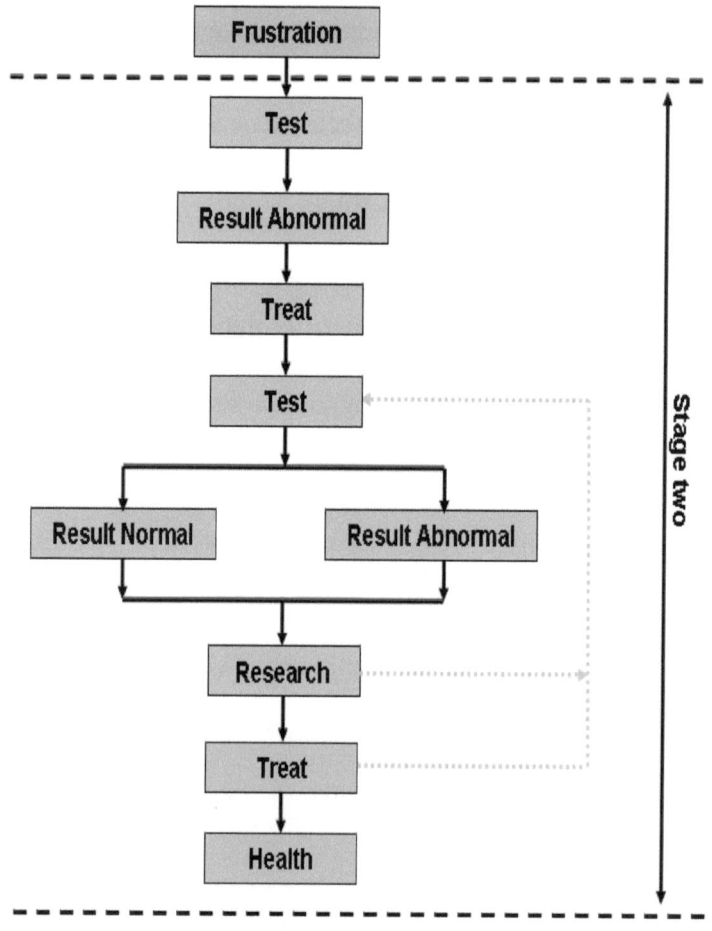

Ignore the doubters who say you can't keep on testing you can and you must

At the point I began to understand my realities I knew my life would change

So that when you're at the other end of your health recovery campaign you can then speak from a platform of assurance, confidence and righteousness. You can challenge the integrity of those who failed you, ignored or abused you, because at that point you're more than an equal for anyone who would choose to play games with you because you're able to ask with assurance:

- Why are we as a nation wasting so much money on fundamentally flawed tests etc., whilst writing people off with impunity?

- Why are some of us, with a desire to be well, having to self research, self fund and self acquire best in class medical and clinical investigations outside the UK?

- Where is the medical establishment when we need it?

- Who within our current appalling medical service sector ranks can dare to defend this level of clinical and administrated incompetence?

I have a magnificent body that supports me in all my endeavours

There really is only one way to ensure that you get through your health predicaments and that is to take control of your stage two process whilst ensuring you stay in total control of your entire health optimisation process re: below.

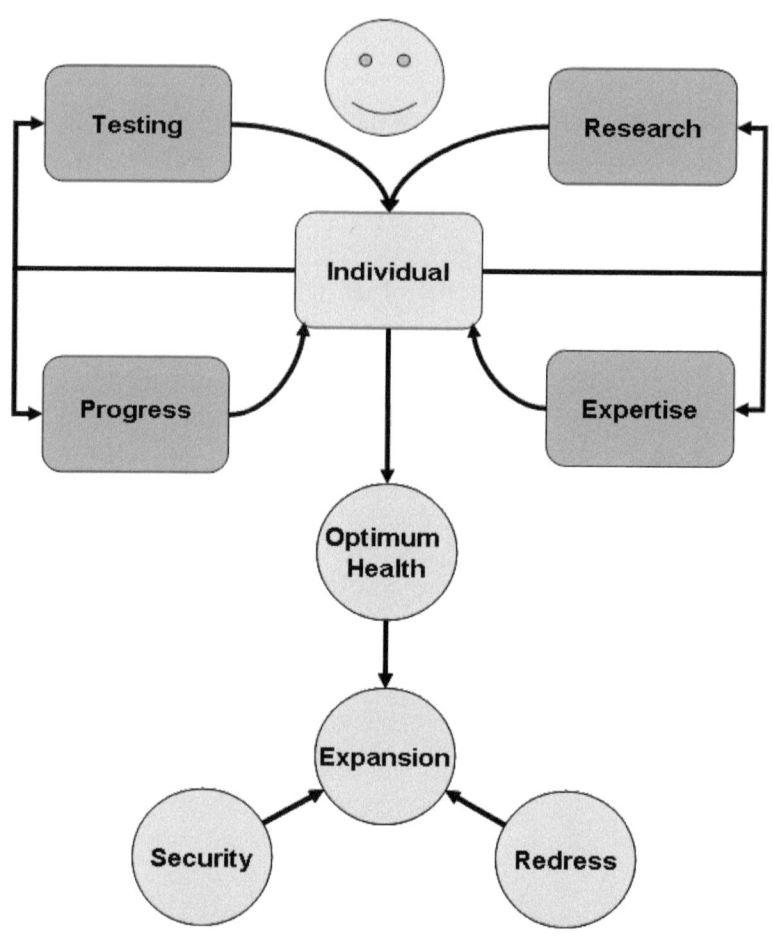

Taking Individual Control of All Health Related Processes

At the point I began to understand my realities I knew my life would change

EXPLORING ANALYTICAL TESTING OPTIONS PRAGMATICALLY

Exploration Twelve

I have a magnificent body that supports me in all my endeavours

At the point I began to understand my realities I knew my life would change

I've made great play throughout this book of the need for effective testing and re-testing if necessary, to enable effective diagnosis of underlying diseased states. Yet whilst those tests can take many forms including: imaging and bodywork. I believe that the key to identifying the root cause of any chronic condition begins with effective blood and biochemical marker analysis. The clinic that I used for my detailed blood analysis via my private GP Dr. Sarah Myhill referrals was 'Biolab Medical Unit UK'.

Biolab Medical Unit is a; medical referral laboratory specializing in nutritional and environmental medicine which is located in the heart of the West End of London. They are a nutritional biochemistry laboratory measuring vitamin and mineral levels, toxic metals, other biochemical levels that are related to the availability of vitamins, minerals and other nutrients. They have an extensive range of profiles for assessing the effects of twenty-first century lifestyles on our bodies and are dedicated to assisting doctor's sort out their patients' problems in a way that does not rely on drugs as a first line of treatment. Biolab apply modern scientific laboratory analytical methods to establish what imbalances there are in the bodies of those who are suffering ill-health or non-optimum health, so that these imbalances may be addressed via nutritional and non-drug means, with the aim of achieving good health or, at least, improving the quality of life and minimizing suffering.

I would therefore suggest that it's worth visiting their website at www.biolab.co.uk/ for a more detailed overview of their services, staff and publications etc. However please note that Biolab Medical Unit (UK) is a referral unit and will only perform tests requested by practitioners registered with;

- The General Medical Council.

I have a magnificent body that supports me in all my endeavours

- The General Dental Council.

- The General Osteopathic Council.

- The General Chiropractic Council.

All test reports will be sent to your practitioner as Biolab will not enter into direct discussions with you about your results, although they are happy to discuss their findings in relation to your tests with your practitioner. It's important to note that I have absolutely no commercial, professional or personal arrangement with Biolab Medical Unit or any other analytical service provider. Furthermore those services providers will be completely unaware of my personal use of their services or my recommendation of their services. I would nevertheless strongly urge any individual suffering from a chronic health condition and wishing to undergo private blood investigations etc., to discuss their case with their medical/clinical service provider and request that they enter into discussions with respective analytical service providers such as Biolab. But be under no illusion that you may find that an uphill battle because medics in general traditionally poo poo anything that deviates from their own ignorant perspectives. If that is the outcome of your discussions then you have only three choices open to you:

(a) Stay with your current service provider.

(b) Secure more appropriate service support.

Or

(c) Give up completely on life.

At the point I began to understand my realities I knew my life would change

Ultimately as the masters of our own health and happiness we must make the choices we feel are best for us and in that we must be prepared to stand or fall, live or die by the choices we choose to make.

I have a magnificent body that supports me in all my endeavours

At the point I began to understand my realities I knew my life would change

Exploring personal mind anger pragmatically

Exploration Thirteen

I have a magnificent body that supports me in all my endeavours

At the point I began to understand my realities I knew my life would change

You know I've encountered many many very special people in my life and I'm incredibly grateful for the interactions that I've had with them all. I've been blessed to meet fine tradesmen, carers, beggars, artists, clergymen, engineers, bus drivers, road sweepers, teachers, librarians, sportsmen etc., to name just a few. Each one special and unique in their own right, each one bringing something special to my life and yet I can count on one hand the medics I've met whom I would bestow the accolade of special upon.

Yet I make no secret of the fact that whilst I will be as gracious as circumstances dictate when interacting with members of the medical industry. I nevertheless have absolutely no respect for that industry or the views of those employed within it for unless I meet a medic who is able to speak or offer a service from a point of true expertise and I don't mean legitimized bullshit. Then I'm simply not interested in what any medic has to say, and I mean, I'm not interested in anything they have to say on health, politics or any major imposition on life.

I have a magnificent body that supports me in all my endeavours

You see, as far as I'm concerned they are the lowest of all mortal forms of life. The way these people conduct themselves, fail and abuse people in their care is a scandal and disgrace and for that I'm adamant that for their crimes against humanity they must pay a very heavy price, be that in this life or the next I really don't care. Until that happens I think its fine to explore in your head exactly what you would do to the rogues who've abused and failed you if you ever got the chance to deliver your own unique and personal retributions.

Now whilst some may say: *'Oh dear it's important for our souls and our recovery that we must let go of hatred and anger towards others'*. My answer is simply this, *'Explore that position again when you're tormented by a toxic liver, a toxic body and when every system and organ in your body has been damaged by an insidious bacteria, when it all could have been so easily prevented'* and then I would urge you to simply think your belief structures over again.

You see I personally believe that it's actually extremely healthy and positive to exercise your liver and brain anger. To explore just how far your emotions take you and what you think is suitable, punishment or not, for the suffering you've endured. Who knows, the very fact that you're prepared to explore those thoughts whilst accepting them for what they are, may just be an essential component of your recovery and a vital process that must not be ignored.

With that point of view in focus, I've had some lovely despicable thoughts about what I would like to do to the rogues who failed me. I so desperately want them to feel the level of pain that they create and perpetuate for people like me every minute of every day of their career. I've had thoughts of rounding all medics and their families up and transferring them to great football stadiums around the country.

At the point I began to understand my realities I knew my life would change

Where I would strap the medics into chairs and make them watch their loved ones being torn apart without mercy by Hyenas. Now obviously that would take some time because there's only so much a Hyena can eat at any given time but that's okay, the longer the suffering for all concerned the better as far as I'm now concerned. You may ask why I chose Hyenas not lions, tigers, wolfs or bears, well it's because of all the big carnivores the Hyena is in my opinion the cruelest of them all. They don't waste energy killing their victims they simply rip them apart limb from limb. I think being eaten alive and enduring unbelievable suffering before death is fine for the sort of people that I have in mind.

Now of course and after a few years naturally there wouldn't be any family or loved ones left to brutalize, so I would turn my attention directly to the medics. At which point I really would enjoy playing mind games with them torturing them day after day for years. I would inject them with all sorts of substances and break the odd one or two limbs. There would be no quarter given, no repose on grounds of mercy.

But I might allow the odd one of two to read a few books on psychology if they felt it would help them deal or cope with their physical and emotional pain. I would inject some with Lymes Disease, some with HIV, some with syphilis and some with a blend of all three. But before all of that I would revel in playing games with their head and simply talk infinitum about a whole host of things I was planning to do.

I have a magnificent body that supports me in all my endeavours

The key in all my punishment regimes would be the generation of intolerable isolation, desolation and despair, creating a situation devoid of any humanistic sympathy or due diligence and care. In fact to replicate the culture that these rogues have rolled out on us for years, only in my regime there would be no 'DSBL's' written, no bullshit spoken and no postulation of care, my open and honest policy would be one of simple retribution and payback for the insidious lives that they'd lived.

Now I'm not sure if my anger towards the medical industry will ever subside but what matter that, all that I know is that I can't possibly allow my hatred of them to hold me back. I'm no longer their victim or some innocent that they can indiscriminately abuse, for I'm now 'Barry Hardy' the battle hardened medic hater who will delight in pursuing legal retribution and in due course regardless of whatever form or format that takes.

You see; I want everyone who's ever been chronically ill yet failed by the medical industry to realise and accept fully that they themselves were never to blame. In accepting that they, like me can exercise the demons that reside deep within us all after years of suffering. Because in accepting and not fighting our mind anger, I firmly believe that we're actually setting ourselves free. Simply because personal exploration as far as I'm concerned is nothing more than an intuitive expansive trait and if we choose to live in expansive state we very often leave our pain and suffering behind.

At the point I began to understand my realities I knew my life would change

Now, let me make myself clear, I would never advocate actual violence against any medical service sector worker, rogues though they are by default. Nevertheless I certainly believe and therefore think that it's healthy and positive to accept and explore our brain and liver anger because it has a vital part to play in anyone's recovery.

My only footnote would be in closing this chapter is; go gentle into that vile place and never allow yourself to be completely consumed by your cruel thoughts, just accept them for what they are.

It really is okay to hate your medical abusers and accept that they are complete 'shits, cretins and clowns'. It's okay to hate their husbands, wives and kids for reaping great rewards from being associated with and/or to those rogues.

The only point I would make is turn that hatred into positive redress and legal action and don't let it just fester or simply evaporate away. Make your formal complaints if that's what you need to do for in doing so you will kick start a myriad of much needed karmic events.

Network with fellow mindsets and empower yourself in firm assurance that you're no longer that lone foot soldier that you'd lead yourself to believe you are, because at the point you empower your psyche to engage in seeking redress, you've morphed into a dynamic and cataclysmic particle of change.

I have a magnificent body that supports me in all my endeavours

That will prove to you once and for all, that you're a very real, dramatic, even majestic vanquisher of what is an insidious blight upon society i.e. our shockingly poor and unresponsive medical model, industry and the shits who work within it who are happy to destroy far too many peoples' lives.

At the point I began to understand my realities I knew my life would change

Exploring your current diagnosis pragmatically

Exploration Fourteen

I have a magnificent body that supports me in all my endeavours

At the point I began to understand my realities I knew my life would change

So; you've read my highly opinionated postulations in terms of the originators and drivers of chronic illness expression, the question now is are you up for testing your historical perceptions. If so let's explore that receptivity in this final chapter.

Do you know there is one sure fire thing about anyone suffering from chronic illness expression including Manic Depression and that is; sufferers will do and take anything they can to remove it from their life. The majority in the end resort to a whole raft of escapist options because living in their body is simply beyond mortal endurance at times. It's not untypical for a sufferer of Manic Depression to indulge and self indulge in a wide range of escapist pursuits some of which include:

- Exercise.
- Deviant acts.
- Drugs.
- Cigarettes.
- Alcohol.
- Orthodox medication.
- Herbal supplements.
- Homeopathy.

And even

- Suicide attempts.

Whilst others commit to

- Suicide completions.

I have a magnificent body that supports me in all my endeavours

Such is the suffering of those, experiencing unrelenting, Manic Depression that for most their only constant thought is that of finding some how or some way of detaching themselves from its grasp. As a former chronic illness sufferer, I know only to well the depth of despair that chronic illness can push you into when there is not a treatment, a medication, a supplement, an activity or self destruct approach that does not remove your major presenting symptoms. I truly know what it's like to live in a body when NOTHING and I mean NOTHING even remotely diminishes the impact of chronic illness upon your entire being. Nevertheless I'm stating firmly for the record that it's possible to lower chronic illness expression rapidly. In fact it's possible to feel better than you've ever felt in your life before, because at the point you address the underlying cause of your illness your recovery profile picks hitherto unthinkable momentum. Yet the approach that I prescribe is unlike any of the majority of orthodox options you may have encounter before because it does not include:

- Self beasting through Psychoanalysis.

Or

- Detachment though 'Somnolence' inducing concoctions.

Or even

- A combination of both ridiculous approaches.

At the point I began to understand my realities I knew my life would change

You see, Raphael's Treatment Protocol RTP is based upon looking at chronic illness expression i.e. Manic Depression objectively and doing your utmost to uncover via root cause analysis the physical generator and/or generators of chronic illness expression before even looking at treating the symptoms of that disease generated diseased state. That is not to say that the sufferer is left in purgatory as is the case with current treatment approaches. Because the diminishment of negative symptom expression within hours is the short term goal of RTP, and that I may add is not some grandiose statement without substance because in reality it will be proven as fact. You see; if your original and/or presenting symptoms are the derivative of disease expression, which there is a great possibility that they are; then very simple, very effective and very safe bodily testing will prove that to you.

Thereafter RTP focuses upon the sustainability of underlying disease eradication whilst supporting the body through effective and re-energized removal of all associated toxic loads from the body. Note however that there are no ridiculous detox regimes in the RTP, no regimes of excessive supplement ingestion, but there is a need for whole body analysis and with that the chronic illness sufferer must accept there is an initial cost.

I have a magnificent body that supports me in all my endeavours

Extract Summary from the Raphael Treatment Protocol

1. You must have access to and be supervised by a suitably qualified practitioner.

2. You must NOT stop any treatment protocol you're currently undertaking until your analysis results have been compiled.

3. You must be prepared to accept that you will have to pay for several highly specialised blood and bodily function tests including:

    i. Mitochondria Analysis.
    ii. Viral Analysis.
    iii. Chlamydia Analysis.
    iv. Lymes Disease Analysis.
    v. Syphilis Analysis.
    vi. Fungal Analysis.
    vii. Methylation Analysis.
    viii. Sulphanation Analysis.
    ix. Thyroid Analysis.

    And

    x. A 24 hour Saliva Adrenal Function test.

4. You must be prepared to look objectively at your results with your practitioner and understand exactly what's happening and/or going on in your body.

At the point I began to understand my realities I knew my life would change

5. You must be prepared to undertake supervised treatment regimes designed to:

    i. Quash any microorganism disease states.
    ii. Support and energize any diseased organ states.
    iii. Support your bodies detoxing capabilities.

6. Monitor your body at every stage of your treatment protocol because as covered in the TBS chapter it's important to know where you're at.

7. Above all be gentle with yourself because the road to recovery is full of ups and downs during the process of disease eradication, toxin removal and whole body system re-energization.

Be under no illusion that at the point you begin to address any underlying disease states and commence the process of bio/lipo toxin removal from your body you will begin to feel much better almost immediately. Thereafter windows of freedom from chronic illness expression will become more frequent until chronic illness expression is nothing more than far a distant episode from your past. Now look I'm not naive to think that anyone reading this chapter will fully understand the point I'm making about my alternative approach to chronic illness eradication. But there is a very simple test that anyone suffering from Manic Depression expression can do if they wish to explore a new way of understanding their condition and I qualify that for you on the next page.

I have a magnificent body that supports me in all my endeavours

Take a small quantity of the suggested products re: below over let's say one to four days. The products I'm referring to are natural yet highly potent and they can be bought online or from any good health food store. All the products I'm about to suggest are antimicrobial, antibacterial and anti-inflammatory which means that they will immediately kill foreign invaders whilst reducing initially some of any directly or indirectly associated inflammation. They are:

- One tea spoon of Higher Nature 'MSM organic Sulphur Crystals' in water morning and night.

Or

- 2-5 drops NutraMedix 'Samento' in water morning and night.

Or

- 2-5 drops NutraMedix 'Cumanda' in water morning and night.

Or

- 2-5 drops Higher Nature 'Citricidal' Grapefruit Seed Liquid Extract in water morning and night.

It should be noted that I have absolutely no commercial or clinical/medical arrangement with either Higher Nature or NutraMedix including any other directly or indirectly associated party. I'm merely citing their products simply because I found them to work well for me.

At the point I began to understand my realities I knew my life would change

If you have an underlying disease which is responsible and/or contributing to your chronic illness expression then the result of taking small doses of the suggested products should be;

1. An immediate lifting in mood and may even move your mood slightly into a hyper or manic mode.

And

2. A reduction in bodily tension and pain and in some instance tension and pain may simply disappear.

However

3. The sufferer's mood will be drastically lowered again within a 8 / 12 hour window and all associated pain will increase with additional pain being generated in new and strange locations.

Now the reason all that happens time after time is because that is the standard Herxheimer Reaction (HR) that people with chronic disease states incur at the point they begin to address their diseased state. It's a toxic reaction generated in the body by toxins being released from dead or decaying parasites, fungus, viruses, bacteria or other pathogens. As these toxins circulate in our body, it is not uncommon to experience flu-like symptoms including headache, joint and muscle pain, body aches, sore throat, general malaise, sweating, chills, nausea or other symptoms. This is normal and indicates that parasites, fungus, viruses, bacteria or other pathogens are being effectively killed off.

The biggest battle we all face in recovering from disease expression via RTP is dealing with the HR in a way that enables us to function and ensure that we can continue to medicate and support our bodies through what is a truly hellish situation. I myself have arrived at that point now because after years of self treating and suffering I've found the formula that allows me to kill my bodily invaders whilst supporting my defective detox capabilities via a number of gentle treatment protocols not least of which includes the use of a far infrared sauna daily. But you can read more about that in my book *Raphael's Treatment Protocol*.

At the point I began to understand my realities I knew my life would change

Now there is one further important point I need to make here in relation to the support of chronic illness suffers who are clearly experiencing some degree of endocrine system insufficiency and that is I completely agree with the medication of small doses of hormones in terms of:

1. Hydrocortisol and/or prednisolone to support the adrenals, *which can be purchased online without a prescription.*

And

2. Synthetic Armour to support the thyroid, *which can be purchased online without a prescription.*

So whilst pompous medics will cry foul on that matter and cite my support of such medications as evidence of my cavalier and ludicrous approach to wellness. All I can say is that in controlled and supervised dosage both medication offer far greater whole body health benefits than many well known prescription medications that are given out willy nilly. In fact they are probably less dangerous when handled with integrity than:

- Alcohol.

- Cigarettes.

- High fat foods.

And

I have a magnificent body that supports me in all my endeavours

- Controlled substances such as:

    I. Crack cocaine.

    II. Heroine.

    III. Marijuana etc.

All off which can be purchased with ease and consumed in completely irresponsibly fashions, all imposing greater harm onto already impoverished capabilities of sufferers with any form of chronic illness. All appear to be addictive and whilst some have a more direct impact upon specific organs, i.e. lungs, brain and liver. Unfortunately cocaine, heroine and marijuana carry a much deadlier addictive tendency and can even damage many areas in the brain not least of which includes Gaba receptors and associated neuro-networks leading to emotional/psychological complications.

Now look I've sort of laboured that point for one very specific reason, and that is if your tests prove you're suffering from adrenal insufficiency there is absolutely no way that a medic will provide you with small dose endocrine system support and so at that point your way forward is entirely up to you. Personally however I say stay well clear of the cigarettes, alcohol, high fat foods, cocaine, heroine and marijuana because they are only for people who've given up on life, so if you've chosen life which I hope you have then cast your net further and explore where you can find the endocrine help and support that you need.

At the point I began to understand my realities I knew my life would change

I really get the hump when I hear 'luddite' medics rattling on about the dangers of endocrine system support and I do so because those very same 'charlatans' every day of their career abuse people in their care by default. On top of that they're only to happy to hand out in buckets or skips whichever is your choice, prescriptions for a whole host of side effect riddle concoctions. The very same concoctions that immediately place you in the:

- Psychiatric treatment trap, with all is shortfalls and associated medical/clinical abuse loops.

And

- Compromise your body's recovery processes further by their highly toxic effects upon your methylation and sulphanation processes............arrrrrrrrrrr they make me so angry.

I have a magnificent body that supports me in all my endeavours

Let me be very clear here I'm in no way advocating that anyone suffering from chronic illness expression should walk away from the supervision and/or treatment protocols they're currently committed to. But what I am saying is that there is a need for a change in perceptions in and about the origin of chronic illness expression and my only hope is that at the very least my postulations enable some form of educated debate. No one should have to live with irresolvable chronic illness it is neither a karmic lesson nor an opportunity to grow. Chronic illness is nothing more than an insidious blight upon our lives and so no matter which way we or anyone from the medical/clinical industry chooses to look at it. The expression of chronic illness in society at large needs to be removed from our society and psyche completely and Amen.

If you do nothing else for the rest of the day after you've read this book I implore you to explore what I have to say from an educated and considered perspective and above all things be gentle with yourself and your body because at the end of the day, that's all we really have at our disposal. May your god and the power of your own force now take you to the place and space within your inner health where you need to go! A place that I hope now presents to you day after day; mortal beauty, hope, inspiration and love.

At the point I began to understand my realities I knew my life would change

AUTHORS NOTES

I have a magnificent body that supports me in all my endeavours

At the point I began to understand my realities I knew my life would change

Personal Insight and Ownership

I'm aware that I've scared and troubled many people in the past with my ability to: analyse, condemn, congratulate and even poke fun at myself in the pursuit of reality and my own personal progression. I'm a very big believer that personal insight and personal ownership of all our mortal endeavours is the key to a truly considered life. Therefore if the tone, substance and/or in-depth of personal expression or certain aspects of my personal life are too much for any of my readers. I would respectfully suggest that perhaps its time for them to stop reading and start writing, for the expression of repression certainly offers release as far as I understand, from the tension we all as mortals appear to manufacture with ease.

Medics and the Medical/Clinical World

The medical world is full of humans each with their own unique gifts, skills and personal flaws and it's because the medical world is full of mortals and not earth God's that they fail us so badly day after day. But don't just sit back any longer when you're abused, let down or failed by anyone in the medical/clinical world. Sue them and bring them and their industry to account if you desire, for in doing so you will not only help yourself via the pursuit of redress, but indirectly you'll play a very big part in helping the entire human race.

I have a magnificent body that supports me in all my endeavours

The Great Psychological Bluff and Scandal

If we allow others to cloud our realities in terms of who we are and what we're actually experiencing with inappropriate postulations about the state of our psychology, be under no illusion we fail ourselves completely at every conceivable level. On matters of psychology when pursuing well-being, listen to your antagonists but choose not to hear when you're being written as another psychological basket case. Because I'm confident you'll discover if you test your body thoroughly, that it's your body that's at fault not your emotions or mind. At that point all psychological assertions can be met head on as you pursue a meaningful life.

Eminently Solvable Conditions

When you're health conditions are being fudged and written off as illnesses that have only names with no treatment or resolution options open or offered to you to help you get by or simply cope. You really have only two options open to you and that is to stick with what you've got if that's all you can do or you can test and test until your condition or conditions are identified. We are all the sole guardians of our own mortality; therefore we can either relinquish our responsibility to the uncaring and obscene or we can fight for what is our mortal right, the right to decency and an acceptable quality of life.

At the point I began to understand my realities I knew my life would change

Depression Expression

There is no insanity at all in depression expression save only for the sheer depth of suffering its victims incur. Because the reality is that depression expression can be eradicated in days, not weeks, months or years when the physical generators, precursors and accelerators of depression expression are treated and removed. All that is needed is a shift in perceptions, a position significantly enhanced by holistic treatment results.

Stressful Resolution

Whilst the majority of us have experienced some degree of stress at some point in our life, very few of us realise that it's so predictable, so treatable and so recoverable from, hence nothing whatsoever for us all to get stressed about. Once you understand the dynamics, your stress levels will fall and at that point you will wonder why you allowed yourself to get so stressed in the first place or indeed at all.

Wellness

There is no great secret to wellness over and above understanding the root cause of any decline from wellness into un-wellness. But that root-cause analysis is not determined by non intrusive subjective analysis, because it can only be determined by holistic, scientific testing and analysis. Anything less than that is mere supposition, supposition however has never cured anyone or created a state of considered wellbeing, but it has forced many poor mortals like you, me and us, to give up completely on the idea of a satisfying mortality. But no longer yeah?

I have a magnificent body that supports me in all my endeavours

Divine or Higher Force

We all at some point need someone or something to pray to, no matter what race or creed we originate from. But the reality is when all said and done, we all as mortals are the only living beings able to solve complex mortal mysteries, so whilst it's okay I suspect to offer up prayers. I think it best that we all put our faith in ourselves and the endeavours of our fellow men.

At the point I began to understand my realities I knew my life would change

Web sites you may wish to explore

The information provided here is for research only; no responsibility will be accepted for the scope or content of any of these web sites.

1. www.doctormyhill.co.uk
2. www.biolab.co.uk/
3. www.thyroiduk.org/
4. www.nutramedix.com
5. www.mickeltherapy.com
6. www.moodcure.com/
7. www.reikifed.co.uk/
8. www.thyroidtears.co.uk/
9. www.paulocoelho.com/ *(My favourite Author)*

OTHER BOOKS BY BARRY HARDY

Further personal insight and self help books written by Barry Hardy in relation to Raphael's Legacy include:

Raphael Treatment Protocol
Stress at Close Quarters
Anxiety at Close Quarters
Exploring Fluid Normality
Arthritis at Close Quarters
Depression at Close Quarters
Fibromyalgia at Close Quarters
Lymes Disease at Close Quarters
Gulf War Syndrome at Close Quarters
Toxic Body Syndrome at Close Quarters
Myalgic Encephalopathy at Close Quarters
Chronic Fatigue Syndrome at Close Quarters
Obsessive Compulsive Disorder at Close Quarters

You can purchase any of these books at www.barryhardy.com

At the point I began to understand my realities I knew my life would change

Decency Warning

This warning is repeated and placed at the back of this book because if you're like my daughter you're sure to start at the back of this book and I certainly don't wish to offend any back book readers either. Therefore please don't read this book if you are easily offended by:

- Strong views.
- Strong language.
- Grammatical inconsistencies and/or poor grammar.

Or

- Personal experiences and perceptions expressed freely.

I have a magnificent body that supports me in all my endeavours

Personal Notes

At the point I began to understand my realities I knew my life would change

Personal Notes

I have a magnificent body that supports me in all my endeavours

Personal Notes

At the point I began to understand my realities I knew my life would change

Personal Notes

I have a magnificent body that supports me in all my endeavours

Personal Notes

At the point I began to understand my realities I knew my life would change

Personal Test Results

I have a magnificent body that supports me in all my endeavours

Personal Test Results

At the point I began to understand my realities I knew my life would change

Personal Treatment Notes

I have a magnificent body that supports me in all my endeavours

Personal Treatment Notes

At the point I began to understand my realities I knew my life would change

Personal Treatment Notes

I have a magnificent body that supports me in all my endeavours

Personal Treatment Notes

At the point I began to understand my realities I knew my life would change